Your Towns and Cities in the Great War

Seaford and Eastbourne
in the Great War

Your Towns and Cities in the Great War

Seaford and Eastbourne
in the Great War

Kevin Gordon

Pen & Sword
MILITARY

First published in Great Britain in 2014 by
PEN & SWORD MILITARY
an imprint of
Pen and Sword Books Ltd
47 Church Street
Barnsley
South Yorkshire S70 2AS

ISBN 978 1 78303 642 4

A CIP record for this book is available from the British Library

Printed and bound in England
by CPI Group (UK) Ltd, Croydon, CR0 4YY

Typeset in Times New Roman by Chic Graphics

Pen & Sword Books Ltd incorporates the imprints of
Pen & Sword Archaeology, Atlas, Aviation, Battleground, Discovery,
Family History, History, Maritime, Military, Naval, Politics, Railways,
Select, Social History, Transport, True Crime, and Claymore Press,
Frontline Books, Leo Cooper, Praetorian Press, Remember When,
Seaforth Publishing and Wharncliffe.

For a complete list of Pen and Sword titles please contact
Pen and Sword Books Limited
47 Church Street, Barnsley, South Yorkshire, S70 2AS, England
E-mail: enquiries@pen-and-sword.co.uk
Website: www.pen-and-sword.co.uk

Contents

Acknowledgements

When I took on the challenge of writing this book about the Great War I sought advice from Brigid Chapman from Lewes, who kindly assisted me.

Paul Waller pointed me towards information about schools during the war and Phil Armstrong and Ben Franks assisted with photographs. All are volunteers at the Seaford Museum Archives. Other photographs have been kindly supplied by Rosemary Holland, Jim Marsh, Peter Mason, East Sussex Libraries and Peter White

Peter Fellows and Norman Franks gave me invaluable information about the early RAF. Lionel Jones and the staff of Eastbourne Library also cheerfully assisted me.

I am particular indebted to Rodney Castleden who edited my writing to manageable proportions. He kindly shared his knowledge as an experienced author of history books.

Lastly, I would like to thank my wife Mandy, for her support and patience.

Introduction

One hundred years ago, the most catastrophic war affected every city, town and village in Britain and had long-lasting global repercussions.

I have always been fascinated by the Great War. The story of my grandfather, Alex Gordon, was one of bravery, excitement and pain. When his leg was blown off during the Zeebrugge Raid on 24 April 1918, he must have suffered terribly but he was always cheerful. Sadly, his experience was not unusual. Everyone in the county had at least one family member or friend who had a similar story of suffering to tell, if they survived, and of course many of them were never to return home.

Although the whole country was embroiled in the war, the coastal towns of Seaford and Eastbourne in Sussex were closer to it than most places. Naval battles could be heard from the towns and sometimes even seen by those who had a good pair of binoculars. Thousands of troops were billeted in the area either in private homes or in massive camps like the two at Seaford.

Sources of information are sometimes difficult for a period that teeters on the brink of human memory. The first-hand sources, the soldiers, have all gone now. The last surviving British soldiers of the Great War, 111-year-old Harry Patch and 113-year-old Henry Allingham, died within a few days of each other in 2009. Henry lived in Eastbourne and died at St Dunstan's Home (Blind Veterans UK) at Ovingdean. Thousands of local men died in the conflict, all with stories to tell, even though today they may have become little more than names on a war memorial. But the story of the war is wider than the story of soldiers. Other groups of people were involved too, such as women and conscientious objectors. The civilian populations of Seaford and Eastbourne had their own very different experience of the Great War.

The primary sources for this book heavily feature contemporary newspapers. Archive material from local museums has been used too. Newhaven Fort, Eastbourne Redoubt and the smaller museums at Seaford and Newhaven proved rich sources of information.

Other books have been written about this stretch of the Sussex coast in the Great War, most notably Bob Elliston's *Eastbourne's Great War*, so this book seeks to avoid unnecessary duplication of coverage. To give another example, the early days of aviation at Eastbourne and the subsequent role of aviation in the Great War have been covered comprehensively in a resource published by the Eastbourne History Society: *The Eastbourne Aviation Company 1911-1924*. For details on early aviation at Eastbourne, the reader is recommended to use that. Other sources for this book are listed in the bibliography.

CHAPTER 1

Prelude to War

A background of conflict

Seaford and Eastbourne have been on the frontier of invasion and conflict for thousands of years. The Roman occupation and the Norman Conquest both made direct impacts on this stretch of the Sussex coast. During the Hundred Years War in the Middle Ages there were frequent assaults by the French.

By the thirteenth century Seaford had become an important port, thanks to the export of wool to the continent. By 1229 it was a Cinque Port, a part of the confederation of south coast ports that supplied ships and men to protect the country prior to the creation of the Royal Navy. Seaford was a limb, a subsidiary port, of Hastings along with nearby Pevensey. French attacks and the Black Death decimated the populations of Eastbourne and Seaford. In 1380, Seaford was given remission from taxes due to the frequency of the French raids. As families moved inland into the safety of the Downs, villages such as Alfriston and Hailsham started to grow. Eastbourne at this time was a small settlement called Bourn, clustered round St Mary's Church, but it still had to contribute. During the reign of Edward III the village was taxed to provide funds to fight the French.

Probably the last invasion attempt on this section of the coast came on 18 July 1545 when a French fleet, under the command of Admiral Claude D'Annebault, landed in Seaford Bay. The local landowner, Sir Nicholas Pelham, was also Commander of Musters in Sussex. It was his responsibility to gather militias and any available local people to fight off the foreigners, and together they succeeded in pushing the French back on to their ships.

In 1587, anticipating a Spanish invasion, a survey of the Sussex coast was made by Sir Thomas Palmere and Walter Covert, who were deputy lieutenants of the county. They reported that at Bourn there was a decayed earthen bulwark and that, although there were cannon, they were 'unfurnished with powdre and shotte'. There were similar earthworks at Newhaven and at Seaford. At nearby Chyngton Farm the gun carriages were 'utterly decayed' and all along the coast it was obvious there was a need for more ordnance. The people of Seaford and Eastbourne must have been in a high state of alert when the Spanish Armada passed along the coast a few months later, on 25 July 1588.

Volunteers needed

The call-up for the Great War was not new to local people. They had been asked before to assist in times of national emergency. In 1612 an enrolment of arms took place in Eastbourne and it is recorded that the vicar at St Mary's, Bourn, and the vicar at St Mary's in Willingdon each had a 'musket furnished'.

On 1 April 1618, Edward, Lord Zouch, who was Lord Warden of the Cinque Ports, appointed William Elfick as captain of the Trained Band at Seaford. The following year Lord Zouch was told at Dover that the men at Seaford had muskets, corslettes, bills and skulls (helmets). They also had five great guns situated in a gun garden. One of the musketeers appears to have been a woman. It is also curious that in those days the military at Eastbourne reported to Chichester while the military at Seaford reported to Dover.

In 1702, the MP for Seaford, William Lowndes, wrote to the Lord Chancellor as Seaford defences had again fallen into disrepair. He complained that the cannon in the gun garden had sunk into the ground and they were so vulnerable that the enemy could take the guns away without anyone knowing, or even turn them round to attack the town.

William Lowndes.

A second muster roll was taken for Seaford in July 1710. Each landowner was required to hold weapons. The thirty-two named men who could bear arms were probably not volunteers. Even so, in May 1794 a former Bailiff of Seaford, Robert Stone, called a meeting in an attempt to recruit sixty men to form a volunteer corps. In just two weeks the necessary number had been found with Thomas Harben as their captain. A similar scheme was started at Eastbourne where barracks were established at South Bourn. In October 1803 a correspondent in Eastbourne noted, 'Everything here is on the alert to receive the enemy.'

Forts against the French

The Napoleonic Wars proved that British distrust of the French was not unfounded. In 1759, John Peter Desmaretz, Architect of the Ordnance, commissioned new defensive batteries at Littlehampton, Brighton, Newhaven, Hastings and Rye, and with two on Seaford Bay.

Within a few months two large batteries were facing out to sea, manned by militia and yeomanry from across the country, forerunners of the soldiers who were to inhabit the camps established in Seaford and Eastbourne during the Great War. During the 1770s and 1780s enemy privateers (officially sanctioned pirate ships) frequently came within range of these guns.

At Blatchington Battery, Colonel Coote Manningham (1765-1809) drew together snipers from a number of regiments to form the 95th Regiment of Foot, later known as The Rifle Corps.

This is the origin of the Rifle Brigade, which saw much action during the

Coote Manningham.

Great War, particularly on the Somme and at Ypres. One cold day in December 1801 an unnamed soldier was buried at East Blatchington Churchyard in Seaford. He was laid to rest in an unmarked grave and the parish register gives only, 'Buried: Soldier ye Rifle Corps.' He was the first of many – at the end of the Great War the Rifle Corps had lost 11,575 men.

Another regiment associated with Seaford is the Honourable Artillery Company. Although based in London, the company chose Seaford as the venue for its annual summer camp. The New Inn was the headquarters and for two weeks each year Seaford was awash with soldiers, rifle practice, marching and practice manoeuvres. The manoeuvres at Seaford helped the regiment prepare itself for war. The company saw action early at the First Battle of Ypres, and at Ancre and Arras, losing over 1,600 men during the course of the war.

In the early 1800s a series of squat round forts known as Martello Towers was built along the south coast with the last two at Eastbourne (Tower 73, known as the Wish Tower) and Seaford (Tower 74, now Seaford Museum). To supplement the towers a large redoubt was built at the eastern end of the Eastbourne Parade. This too is a museum.

Martello Tower 74. (Seaford Museum)

More volunteers

The Sussex Royal Engineer Volunteers were established at Eastbourne in May 1892 led by Captain Frederic Walter Savage, the founder and headmaster of Seaford College. C Company was based in Seaford under Captain Savage. A year earlier in 1891 he had established the Seaford College Cadet Corps. Seven of his boys were enrolled, though they were not issued with guns.

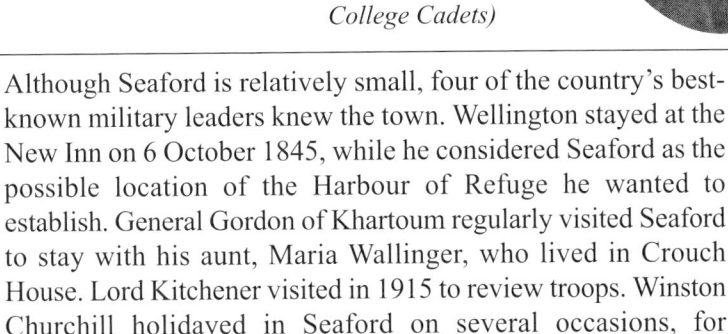

Captain Savage. (Seaford College Cadets)

Although Seaford is relatively small, four of the country's best-known military leaders knew the town. Wellington stayed at the New Inn on 6 October 1845, while he considered Seaford as the possible location of the Harbour of Refuge he wanted to establish. General Gordon of Khartoum regularly visited Seaford to stay with his aunt, Maria Wallinger, who lived in Crouch House. Lord Kitchener visited in 1915 to review troops. Winston Churchill holidayed in Seaford on several occasions, for example in 1911, as his wife Clementine was educated there.

Pre-War camps

The Downs above Eastbourne were often used for military manoeuvres and exercises by various regiments. Whitbread Hollow towards Beachy Head was a favourite venue, as was the land immediately to the north of Seaford – Blatchington Camp.

Camp at Whitbread Hollow.

Two pieces of military equipment used during the Great War were pioneered in Seaford, the train-gun and the means of aerial reconnaissance.

In 1894 a track was laid between Seaford and Newhaven to run a large gun mounted on a railway carriage. The gun, a 40lb breech-loaded Armstrong, was known as the Flying Martello Tower and was the work of the Sussex Royal Engineer Volunteers.

The gun was mounted on a turntable, which men could manoeuvre by pushing round poles inserted into a capstan. The gun was shielded behind a large armoured turret, which had a porthole cut into it to allow the range and direction to be determined. The gun-train was built at the London Brighton & South Coast Railway works in Brighton by Mr R. J. Billington, who was assisted by Colonel Pollock of the Royal Artillery.

The idea was to have mobile guns mounted on railway carriages on tracks on three stretches of the Sussex coast: from Littlehampton to Brighton; from Newhaven to Seaford; and from Pevensey to Hastings.

Train Gun.

The guns could be used to counter the gun-boats of an invader. Although train-mounted guns were not used again along the south coast they were used elsewhere by both sides in the conflict. By the end of the Great War, the Germans' Paris Gun (the biggest gun to be used in the war) was able to bombard the French capital from over 75 miles away.

The balloonist Henry Coxwell was a pioneer of aerial reconnaissance and is believed to have been one of the first people to take photographs from a balloon. He lived in Cinque Ports Road and later Connaught Road in Seaford, and he had a balloon factory in Richmond Road. He was a determined advocate of the use of balloons for aerial reconnaissance and bombing. During the 1860s he petitioned the British army and navy to consider using torpedo balloons, but his ideas fell on deaf ears. During the Franco-Prussian War (1870-1) he was managing war-balloons – for the Germans.

Coxwell's Balloon Factory.

The Boer War

The Boer War, between 1899 and 1902, was probably the first war in which the British people were kept informed of events at the front line in a war far away. Following the relief of Mafeking, patriotic parades were held throughout Sussex and in Seaford the men of C Company of the Royal Engineers pulled a 12-pounder field gun around the town to cheers. The siege of Mafeking was the last conflict in which a Sunday truce was called. The opposing troops regularly met to play cricket.

Men from Eastbourne and Seaford were shipped to South Africa to take part in the action, including several constables from Eastbourne Police Station. Seven men from Seaford were killed in the Boer War and their names were later inscribed on the War Memorial when it was erected for the fallen of the Great War in 1921.

Preparation for war

The Secretary of State for War between 1912 and 1914 was John Seely who, when in Sussex, lived at Blatchington House, Seaford. Seely was responsible, with Sir John French, for arranging army manoeuvres in 1912. These took place in Norfolk and were to be the last major army exercises prior to the war. King George V attended as did General Foch of France, Grand Duke Nicholas of Russia and Field Marshal Jan Smuts from South Africa.

The exercise did not bode well. One of the two teams – the Red Army – was led by Lieutenant-General Sir Douglas Haig, whose army consisted of regular soldiers, staff and cavalry from Aldershot. To their embarrassment they were soundly beaten by a scratch army led by Lieutenant-General Sir James Grierson. Grierson was obviously the more competent commander of the two, but he died of a heart attack a few days after war was declared. Despite his shortcomings during the exercise, it was Haig who would go on to lead the army in the coming war. During the exercise, Seely and the king witnessed a fist-fight between Smuts and the Canadian Minister of Defence. They were brawling over whose men were better.

As a cavalryman Seely believed that horses would be the key to victory. In 1909 he wrote to Lord Haldane, his predecessor as Minister of War, saying 'We do not consider aeroplanes will be of any possible use for war purposes', and in 1913 when the Royal Navy asked for support for their airship project he said, 'Money could be better spent on horses. One horse is worth more than two airships.'

Seely was a friend of Winston Churchill and they may have met during Churchill's holiday visits to Seaford. Although he resigned as Minister of War in 1914, Seely remained active in the military and served most of the war at the Front. He was the only member of the cabinet to have such a close association with the front line and, at Moreuil Wood in France on 30 March 1918, mounted on his horse Warrior, he led one of the last cavalry charges in history.

The exploits of Seely and his exceptional horse were published as *Galloper Jack*, a book that inspired the popular play and film *Warhorse*.

John Seely.

Living on the brink of war

When the Great War broke out, Seaford and Eastbourne were accustomed to being on the front line at times of national crisis. They were by now also growing towns. In 1911, Seaford was still quite small with a population of only 3,683, but Eastbourne's population had grown to 52,542.

Suburban development was just beginning at Seaford. In 1913, 700 acres of land between East Blatchington and Bishopstone were auctioned for housing by the East Blatchington Estate Company. The expansion required a new gasworks to be built and the council purchased the Salts and Blatchington Pond to be used for recreational purposes. The Empire Cinema in Sutton Road opened its doors in May 1913 and a new church was proposed in Wilmington Road.

As a resort, Seaford would never be able to compete with elegant Eastbourne to attract tourists. Instead, dozens of schools sprang up including the huge King's Mead School, which was completed just before the war. The schools of Seaford and Eastbourne were to provide many of the young men who would fight in the war.

The Downs Leisure Centre in Seaford was then a girls' school. The school journals reveal that the girls were politically aware and that they were encouraged to read newspapers and discuss current affairs. They

Downs School, Seaford.

had an active debating society and the subjects for discussion changed significantly during 1913 and 1914. Debates such as 'Are needles more useful than pins' and 'It is better to ride a horse astride than side-saddle' gave way to topics such as 'The substitution of oil for coal in the Royal Navy would be a welcome change' and 'The life of a soldier is preferable to the life of a sailor'. In September 1914 they were debating whether 'Conscription would be of more benefit to England than voluntary service'.

In Eastbourne, the council was committed to creating more housing for the working classes and in 1913 agreed to buy two sites from the Duke of Devonshire. Ten acres around the Archery Pub were to have 154 houses built and another site off Victoria Drive was earmarked for eighty-two houses.

The Suffragette movement was beginning to gather momentum. The Women's Social and Political Union had members in Eastbourne and the town had a branch of the Women's Freedom League. There were many speeches but some action was more militant. On 15 May 1913 the organ at St Anne's Church, Eastbourne, was set on fire and the words 'Vote Vote Vote' were scratched on a nearby memorial. Later that same year two fake bombs were left at the town hall, outside the office of the chief constable of the Eastbourne Borough Police. At the start of the war, the energy of many of these militant women was channelled into supporting the war effort.

War was brewing in Eastern Europe but people in Sussex felt secure enough. In Britain generally there was confidence that the British fleet was the largest and strongest military force in the world. The Royal Navy had 200 destroyers, 150 cruisers, thirty battleships and eighteen dreadnoughts.

On 17 May 1913, HMS *London* made an unscheduled stop off the coast of Eastbourne where the captain's daughter was a pupil at Clovelly-Kepplestone School in Meads. The following day the girls and staff from Clo-Kep School (as it was affectionately known) were invited to join the crew on board the ship where they had luncheon and played deck games. The captain, Ernest Grafton, was promoted to rear-admiral during the war, while HMS *London* would later see action at Gallipoli.

The Grand Fleet
In July 1914, Eastbourne was given a rare treat when there was a visit by a squadron of eight battleships from the Grand Fleet. Excitement grew as the local newspapers showed pictures of the ships that were due to visit shortly before the king's spectacular review of the Grand Fleet at Spithead.

The naval visit gave a real boost to the town's economy with people travelling long distances to see the ships. Exeter Working Men's Club chartered a train to bring them from Devon to see the spectacle. Residents were asked by the mayor, Councillor Bolton, to decorate their houses to mark the occasion.

The ships arrived off Eastbourne at 9.30am on Friday 4 July: the two-year-old battleship, HMS *Marlborough*, the battleships HMS *St Vincent*, HMS *Hercules*, HMS *Superb* and HMS *Vanguard,* and the dreadnoughts HMS *Colossus*, HMS *Collingwood* and HMS *Neptune*. These eight ships were anchored a mile off Eastbourne beach and were brilliantly lit up at night. By day the ships were open to the public for inspection from 1.30pm to 6pm. Hundreds of sailors in uniform came ashore to be treated to a meat tea at the town hall in Grove Road

Fleet off Eastbourne.

followed by entertainments in the drill hall. There were in all 1,250 sailors on the ships and it was noted in the local press that one of them, on HMS *Collingwood,* was Prince Albert, the future George VI.

The following day Vice-Admiral Sir Lewis Bayly from HMS *Marlborough* had lunch with the mayor at the town hall. A guard of honour was given by the newly established Baden-Powell Scouts. In the afternoon there was a cricket match between Eastbourne Cricket Club and the Fleet. Other events included a Grand Naval Fete at Devonshire Park and aeroplane flights from the Eastbourne Aerodrome near St Anthony's Hill to the east of the town.

HMS *Marlborough*, HMS *St Vincent*, HMS *Colossus*, HMS *Superb* and HMS *Collingwood* were all to see action at the Battle of Jutland in 1916, but there was a more immediate pre-occupation as the fleet set sail for Folkestone. After the fleet left Eastbourne it was found that a black-and-white cat called Tobby had gone missing. It was believed that it had stowed away on board one of the ships. Vice-Admiral Bayly sent out a general signal for the ships of the squadron to be searched. Tobby was later found safe and well, at home in Eastbourne.

There was still plenty in Eastbourne to distract residents from events on the European mainland.

The Sussex Agricultural Society held a show in the town on land at the junction of Paradise Drive and Summerdown Road (now Eastbourne College Memorial Ground) close to where a few months later the Summerdown Camp was to be built.

In July Eastbourne was visited by dozens of foreign journalists invited by the Federation of British Health and Holiday Resorts. The mayor held a garden party for them at Devonshire Park, there was a banquet at The Grand Hotel and then they all went on a coach trip to visit Hampden Park and Beachy Head. Within a matter of weeks those journalists, many of whom were from France and Belgium, would find more pressing things to report on, but that summer it was business as usual on the Sussex coast.

Among the summer visitors that year were Her Majesty the Queen of Greece and her sister HRH Princess Frederic Charles of Hesse, formerly Princess Margaret of Prussia. Their brother was none other than the German Emperor, Wilhelm II. They took rooms at the Grand Hotel. The queen was accompanied by her daughters Princesses Eirene and Catherine and she had stayed at the Grand Hotel before, sometimes with her husband King Constantine. Their son Prince Paul was at Eastbourne College. Then, on 31 July the royal party decided to leave Eastbourne for Folkestone and leave England to return to Greece, their visit having been, as it was expressed, 'curtailed by the crisis'.

Fleet off Eastbourne.

CHAPTER 2

The First Weeks of the War

The Times editorial on 1 August 1914 tried to calm the population: 'Every one can do something to help in a great war. Those who cannot fight must learn to sit still. Those who flock to withdraw balances from banks, or amass stores of food in their houses or rush about the country to seek sanctuary, directly injure their country's cause.' Even before it began, *The Times* knew it was going to be a 'great war'.

On Wednesday 6 August, two days after Britain declared war on Germany, an editorial that seems to put the interests of Eastbourne ahead of those of the nation appeared in the local press:

EASTBOURNE AND THE WAR

The crowds in Eastbourne on Bank Holiday were larger than ever. It is unnecessary to hazard an opinion as to the effect that the War will have on the season. No man can predict with any degree of accuracy what course the struggle may take and it is equally impossible to forecast its duration. Under such circumstances it is the duty of all citizens to do their utmost to advance the interests of the town, to encourage business and find as much employment as possible for the workers.

The Mayor (Councillor C. W. Brown) gained experience during troublesome times in India and is ready and willing to be of service. He will have the assistance of an Emergency Committee. This is no time for obstructiveness or selfish indifference.

The local press was more interested in Eastbourne's need for an all-year-round orchestra than it was in military recruitment.

The *Eastbourne Herald* of 12 August did, however, have a few items concerning the war. There was a report that at Birling Gap the local boy scouts had been tasked with keeping a twenty-four-hour watch on the transcontinental telegraph, laid between Sussex and Dieppe in 1861.

Car owners were asked to put their vehicles at the disposal of the authorities and a Lady Motorist Ambulance Corps was announced for ladies who drove their own cars. This was organised by Miss Frankie Browne of Clovelly-Kepplestone School in Meads. Sixteen ladies enrolled and each car was equipped with medical supplies and a trained nurse. They were to serve the Eastbourne Division of the British Red Cross Society.

The Suffragettes were never slow to seek publicity but realized that continued attacks on the establishment would not assist their cause in wartime. The secretary of the Eastbourne Women's Suffrage Society wrote an open letter to the mayor offering the services of its members on any committee and to assist in any way. Shortly afterwards their opposition, the National League for Opposing Women's Suffrage, which had formed in 1910, announced that they would abandon their propaganda war against the Suffragettes.

The Eastbourne Red Cross established a committee to co-ordinate supplies and appealed for clothing that was 'large enough to fit a six foot man'. Whether this would be used for soldiers or for the expected refugees is not clear. The Red Cross also co-ordinated beds and accommodation. The Eastbourne Free Church Nursing Committee unanimously agreed to make available fifty beds for wounded soldiers who might return to the town.

The call-to-arms
There were three aspects of the call up: the return to duty of reservists;

Eastbourne Borough Police in 1912.

the re-grouping of reservist troops who were out on manoeuvres; and the recruitment of new volunteers. Together they made the call-to-arms. At the same time local volunteer groups were forming including the Eastbourne Home Defence Corps, which consisted of 270 men of the Eastbourne Rifle Club. They already had access to firearms and were practising at the Open Firing Range on the Crumbles. Eastbourne Borough Council allowed its employees to enlist. One hundred and thirty-nine men enrolled, including twenty members of the Borough Police Force. The council agreed to keep their positions open for them at the end of the war.

Some men left highly paid jobs to join up, causing financial hardship for families left without a breadwinner. As soon as the war started the Prince of Wales (later to become Edward VIII) established a fund to relieve this hardship. There was a strong response, with donations coming from not only the affluent but from factory workers and congregations across the country. The Grand Hotel in Eastbourne donated £525. Virtually every pub had a collection box on the bar as did many shops. The Football Association even suggested that the takings for football matches should go towards the fund, but by September the Amateur Football Association had decided to abandon all competitions and for a football battalion to be formed. Eastbourne Borough Council co-ordinated the national fund and started a local fund to provide for what was called civil distress, but in the end very few local problems were experienced.

Recruitment

On 6 August 1914, Kitchener made his famous request to the nation for volunteers. In response to his great call-to-arms, nearly half-a-million men signed up straight away, overwhelming the recruiting offices and the military training facilities. Recruitment was rapid in the early weeks of the war. Unemployment was certainly a key reason to join up, but there was also a wave of patriotic enthusiasm and a feeling among some men that they wanted to see action in case the war ended soon. By the end of September, 750,000 men had joined up, at this stage all volunteers. A mass of advertising urged men to enlist.

Southdowns recruiting poster showing Sussex under attack from Zeppelins.

The recruiting office for the area was at the army compound in Seaside, Eastbourne, but the army did not wait for men to turn up. There were recruiting drives in most of the local towns and villages. Posters and patriotic displays appeared in the local shops and every opportunity to recruit young men was explored. On one occasion early in the war in 1914 twenty-eight new recruits handed in their names at the central bandstand in Eastbourne where there had been a patriotic display and a programme of military music. The *Manchester Guardian* said that these patriotic events at Eastbourne attracted 'all classes of visitor'.

Central Bandstand, Eastbourne.

Call-to-arms Eastbourne.

The excitement of the war caused many boys to enlist. Many wanted to escape the boredom of agricultural work. Sixteen-year-old Harold Pelling worked as a carpenter's lad at Offham. His elder brother William had become a recruiting sergeant and returned to the village to try to persuade his friends to join up, perhaps a bit of strategic thinking on the army's part. Harold was determined to join up and went to the recruiting office in Watergate Lane, Lewes. He lied to the sergeant major there, saying he was seventeen. He was told to go outside and come back in again. The sergeant major told him, 'When I ask how old you are, you are *nineteen*!' Harold served for the duration in the Sussex Royal Garrison Artillery, and he was with friends. His commanding officer was Lieutenant Beard, the son of the local brewery, and his sergeant, Fred Hendy, was the captain of his village football team. After months in Dover his unit was transferred to the Ypres Salient and after surviving gas attacks he was injured by shrapnel from a British gun.

Harold was too young. Others were considered too short for service. William Gallard of Firle Road in Eastbourne managed to join the Royal

Sussex Regiment, but only after being rejected on account of his height no fewer than five times. He served as Private G/5435 and was killed in action in France on 12 January 1916. This fastidiousness at the recruiting offices waned as the death toll at the Front mounted. By the autumn of 1916, 100 men at the camp at Bexhill were passed fit for service abroad in just five minutes.

One of the oldest men in the army, a 64-year-old drill instructor at Eastbourne, had thirty-five years earlier been one of the soldiers who marched 300 miles across Afghanistan prior to the Battle of Kandahar. He rejoined the Shropshire Light Infantry at the start of the war and was promoted to sergeant.

Lowther's Lambs

Claude Lowther was the Unionist MP for Eskdale. He served in the Boer War and was recommended for the Victoria Cross. He was also very rich. In 1911 he moved to Sussex after purchasing the dilapidated Herstmonceux Castle.

He urged Parliament to introduce military conscription and for civilians to be forced to work in industry too. On 9 September 1914 he started his own recruiting campaign along the south coast. Recruiting

Call-to-arms Seaford.

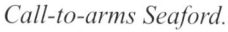

Lowthers Lambs – The Seaford contingent at Cooden Training Camp.

offices were established and when the Eastbourne office opened in Terminus Road there was a long queue of men waiting. Photographs show recruits in Seaford lined up in Broad Street

Within just two days over a thousand men had volunteered. The men were sent to Cooden to train and became the 11th, 12th and 13th Battalions of the Royal Sussex Regiment. They were affectionately nicknamed Lowther's Lambs. One photo shows the Seaford men at Cooden posing with a lamb.

Council tasks and national registration

In 1915, tales of hardship from the Front reached England and the number of volunteer recruits dropped sharply. In July that year the National Registration Act was passed requiring local councils to maintain registers of all men between the ages of 15 and 65. Eastbourne's town clerk used volunteers to compile the Eastbourne list.

The Local Government Board set up in 1871 was abolished in 1919. The board co-ordinated local government across the country and was responsible for a raft of administration, including registration of births, marriages and deaths, public health and town improvements.

During the war the Local Government Board required councils to establish tribunals to consider applications from men who wished to avoid military service. These were usually on the grounds of sickness, indispensability and religion (see Chapter 7). In March 1917 a man with eleven children, all under the age of 15, was exempted from service by the Seaford tribunal on the grounds that, with a separation allowance of 49 shillings a week, he would cost the army too much to employ.

One of the tasks of the local tribunal was to ensure that men working for starred industries (essential to the maintenance of the country) were not enlisted. It was also the tribunal's task to encourage companies to employ women in order to release men to enlist. The expenses of the tribunal were paid from central government funds. There was concern in 1918 that one of the members of the tribunal at Eastbourne was an ex-serviceman. The matter was mentioned in Parliament but it was decided that 'no general action' was required and presumably he continued to serve.

One of the starred industries in Eastbourne was the Motor Omnibus Works in the Roselands area of Eastbourne. The site is now the curiously named Ecmod Road. Ecmod is an acronym for Eastbourne Corporation Motor Omnibus Depot.

Eastbourne is acknowledged as being the first place in the world to run a municipal bus service, opening a fourteen-seat bus service between the Railway Station and Meads on 12 April 1903. Many bus drivers, mechanics and conductors enlisted, and by 1915 the works depot itself joined up, to manufacture shells and other munitions. This helped the war effort and made a profit, which went back into the local economy.

By Christmas 1914, 329 men from Seaford were serving in the military and their names were listed in the local press. Of the 329, ninety-one had joined the Sussex Fortress Royal Engineers, seventy had joined the Royal Sussex Regiment and forty-six men had joined the navy. Only two were in the RAF.

In 1917 the Eastbourne workhouse ceased offering further work to homeless people, deciding that no men of working age in the area should be unemployed. But one of the guardians of the workhouse was so annoyed that the workhouse master had not volunteered for war work that she offered to drive a motor-plough in an attempt to embarrass him into volunteering. Women exerted considerable pressure on their menfolk to enlist.

The 1914 truce
The well-documented Christmas truce of 1914 was witnessed by a local lad, Rifleman R. Barrow of the Queen's Westminsters. Prior to the war

he worked at Bannister & Sons, a clothes shop in Newhaven. He was also a member of the Church Lads Brigade.

In a letter sent back to Newhaven he recalled how on Christmas Eve he was in a trench 200 yards from German lines. (He was between Frelinghien and Houplines on the French-Belgian border.) From 6pm the guns and sniping stopped and he could hear the enemy shouting Christmas greetings and singing carols. At 8pm one brave German stood up and walked across no-man's-land holding a bottle of wine. He was met by an Englishman with a Christmas cake and the two shook hands and exchanged gifts. This fraternization led to more soldiers, including Rifleman Barrow, meeting between the lines. He exchanged small gifts, including cigarettes and buttons, and received a German cigar. He even got the names and addresses of two German soldiers in order to keep in touch after the war.

The truce lasted throughout Christmas Day and in the afternoon Germans left their trenches carrying spades to bury ten of their comrades who had fallen amongst the wire. They were met by a party of English Tommies who helped them bury their dead. Barrow said the truce on his section of the line lasted until 4am on Boxing Day, when his brigade was relieved.

Truce memorial.

CHAPTER 3

The War at Sea

The first attacks

To call the lifeboatmen to duty, two loud maroons and flares would be fired. The people of Eastbourne knew the sound well and young men gathered at the lifeboat-station to help push the lifeboat out across wooden sleepers into the sea.

At 2pm on 23 February 1915, the lifeboat was launched to assist a government collier, the *Branksome Chine* en route from Grimsby to Portsmouth. It was off Beachy Head when it was torpedoed by the German submarine U-8. The Eastbourne lifeboat arrived through choppy waters to see the collier listing with coal tipping out of a hole in its side. Nearby a steamship, the *Oakby*, en route from London to South Wales, had been hit by the same submarine. The crews of both vessels were saved. People gathered on Eastbourne Pier to watch the thick columns of smoke rising from the scene of the double attack. The war at sea, off the Sussex coast, had begun in earnest and was visible to people in the two towns.

Eight other ships had been torpedoed in the previous five days. The press reported these incidents as *pirate* attacks. The terminology clearly looked back to the days of the Napoleonic Wars. The sources of the information are interesting: a special correspondent in Eastbourne and a press release from the German government saying that one of their submarines had sunk 'English transport ship number 192 off Beachy Head'.

The pirates responsible for these attacks were Kapitan-Leutnant A. Stoch and his crew, and the following day they had three more allied

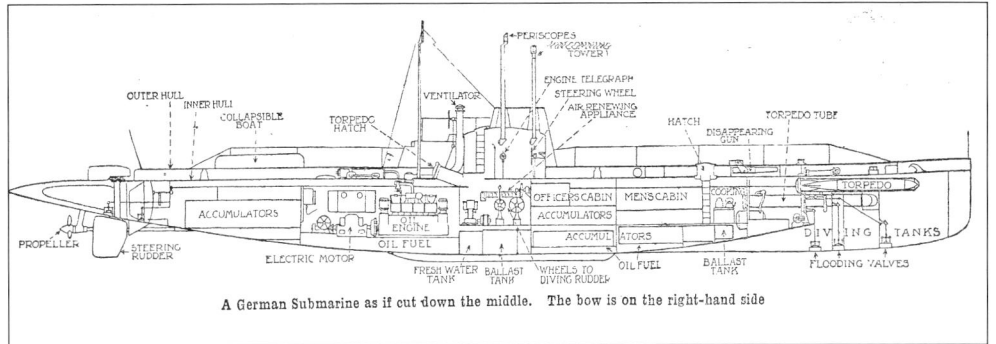

A German Submarine as if cut down the middle.   The bow is on the right-hand side

German submarine plan.

ships in their periscope sights: the *Western Coast*, the *Harpalion* and the *Rio Parana*. The torpedoed *Harpalion* tried to make for the coast but sank and three Chinese members of the crew were drowned. At 5,866 tons, this was one of the largest vessels to have been sunk in British waters thus far.

The torpedoing of English shipping was raised in the House of Commons the next day when there was a call for captured U-boat crews to be dealt with as criminals rather than prisoners-of-war. The prime minister declined to do this, which was lucky for Kapitan-Leutnant Stoch. A week later he, his submarine and crew were captured off Dover.

The spring offensive

On 9 March 1915, another German submarine, U-35, sank a French trawler, the *Griznez*, and the steamer *Blackwood* off the Sussex coast. The crews of both ships were saved and landed at Newhaven. Captain Vogwell of the *Blackwood* was furious. The U-boat had given him no warning beforehand and afterwards surfaced to watch the results of the attack. The German crew could clearly be seen laughing and making no effort to assist as they watched the British sailors boarding lifeboats.

These attacks and the attacks on a further five ships sunk off Beachy Head were widely reported in the press. Most of the ships were torpedoed, although the steamship *Medea* was sunk by U-28 by means of gunfire.

Kapitan Schmidt of the U-28 met his death in an unusual and melodramatic way. After an attack the German submarine got too close to the *Olive Branch* which, despite its name, was carrying ammunition and military vehicles. The U-28 surfaced to survey the damage it had caused. Then a huge explosion sent an army lorry flying through the air. It landed directly on top of the conning tower, crushing Kapitan Schmidt.

On 31 March 1915, the French ship *Emma*, laden with ballast, was torpedoed and sunk by U-boat U-37 a few miles off Beachy Head. U-37 loitered off Eastbourne and the following day was responsible for sinking the *Seven Seas,* a steamer en route from London to Liverpool. Although nine crew members were rescued by the Newhaven lifeboat, the skipper, Captain Barnes, was lost, as were Chief Engineer Jaffa, second mate Henry Hawkes and 70-year-old Steward Charles Wiseman. Four others also lost their lives but the only body to be recovered was that of first mate John Glover, who is buried at Newhaven Cemetery. The *Seven Seas* was the last victim of U-37. Two days later it struck a mine off Dover and the entire crew, including Kapitan Leutenant Erich Wilke, were lost.

The next ship to be sunk off Eastbourne was the steamer *Northlands* on 5 April. It was sunk by U-boat U-33, whose Captain, Konrad Gansser, was far more successful with ninety-three ships to his name. The *Northlands* was en route to Middlesbrough when, at 11.10am, U-33 surfaced behind it. The captain tried to outrun the German submarine by zig-zagging eastwards but the enemy sub easily overtook the *Northlands* and signalled 'Stop or I shall open fire'. The crew of the *Northlands* were ordered to abandon ship and within minutes it was sunk by a single torpedo. The crew were later rescued.

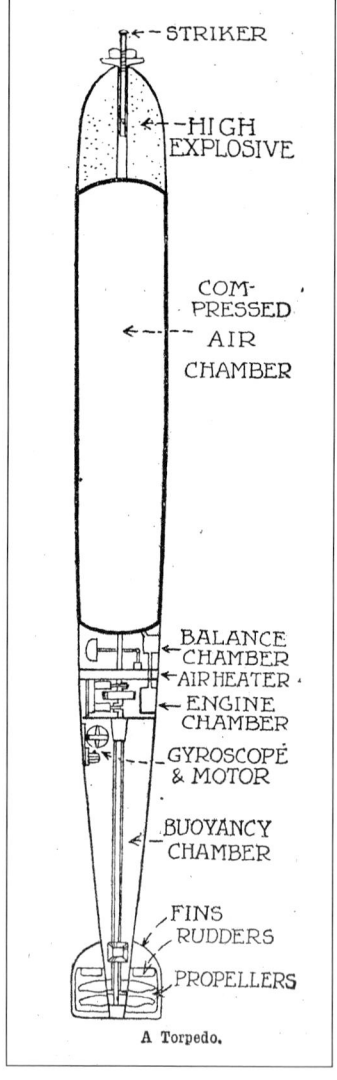

A Torpedo.

A torpedo.

The strategic port of Newhaven and the ships that used it were vulnerable to enemy attack. The Royal Navy acted by seeking to protect the area with torpedo boat destroyers. These heavily armed vessels had been in use since the 1890s and by the end of the war were known simply as destroyers.

A young schoolgirl in Seaford witnessed one of these ships in action and the following poem was later published in the school magazine:

> *I woke to hear the sound of guns –*
> *My window panes were shaken –*
> *And thought I to myself "These Huns*
> *Our Seaford must have taken"*
>
> *I straightaway rose, and cast my glance*
> *Right out upon the sea –*
> *And while I yet seemed in a trance*
> *Appeared – a T.B.D.!*
>
> *Now was fulfilled my greatest hope,*
> *For in the distance far*
> *I did perceive – a periscope!*
> *Oh horrors dire of war!*
>
> *I saw the lovely vessel bright*
> *With evident endeavour*
> *Take a sharp turning to the right*
> *(I thought with pride – "How clever")*
>
> *A white line on the water's crest!*
> *Shot at her from the foe!*
> *Where will the missile come to rest?*
> *Can she ram the sub – or no?*
>
> *Glued on the sea, my eyes I strain –*
> *For telescopes I long –*
> *When – what was that? – my hopes were vain –*
> *The summons of the gong!*

I told my tale, with thrilling pride –
And learnt – that what I'd seen,
Was a practice – (how my fervour died)!
With an English submarine ...

1916 losses

There were no more attacks on shipping off the Seaford-Eastbourne coast for over a year, but on 7 April 1916, the steamer *Braunton* was heading from Boulogne to South Wales with a cargo of empty brass shell cases when she was torpedoed and sunk by U-29. The German submarine offensive against allied shipping continued in the autumn when, on 3 September off Beachy Head a Norwegian ship, the *Gotthard,* was attacked and sunk by U-25.

On 19 October the RMS *Alaunia* was en route from New York to London with 188 passengers when it struck a German mine that had been laid earlier in the day by a German mine-laying submarine UC-16 near the Royal Sovereign Lightship. There was an explosion and two members of the crew, 42-year-old second steward Charles Morris and 16-year-old Trimmer Joseph White, were killed. Despite an attempt to beach the damaged ship it later sank, but not before the rest of the crew and all the passengers were safely landed.

On 21 October U-Boat U-29 sank three ships off Beachy Head. The first was *Fart 3,* which was carrying coal from South Wales to France.

SS Alaunia.

A short time later UB-29 surfaced close to the motor barge *Grit,* which was en route from France to London. A single shot was fired and the captain brought the vessel to a halt. The sea was quite rough at the time so the Germans did not attempt to board. The barge was sunk by sixteen shells and the crew were later rescued by a naval patrol vessel and landed at Newhaven.

The third ship attacked was the *Princess May,* which the crew of UB-29 scuttled by laying explosive charges on board. The following day the steamer *Fortuna* struck a German mine off Eastbourne and went down with fifteen crew.

On 5 November, the *Oushla*, a cargo ship, foundered under the cliffs at Crowlink. Although this could not be put down as a war loss it is

Oushla and submarine 1919.

interesting because it remained *in situ* for many years. In 1919 it was struck by a German U-Boat, U-121, which was being towed to Cherbourg after it had been seized under the War Reparation Scheme. It broke loose in heavy seas, initially ramming the *Oushla*'s boiler room. Later the submarine worked free, but it remained alongside the wrecked steamer for many years until it was salvaged for scrap in 1959.

More regular patrols of the channel by airships and sea-planes meant that shipping losses fell after 1916.

The Newhaven to Dieppe ferry

Being the shortest route between London and Paris it is not surprising that the sea-route between Sussex and Normandy was popular. The first regular cross channel services were between Brighton and Dieppe in the late eighteenth century, however, with the coming of the railway in the mid-nineteenth century, the harbour at Newhaven became the main ferry-port.

In May 1914 a conference was held in Paris where it was decided to improve ferry services between Newhaven and Dieppe. However, these plans had to be abandoned due to the necessities of war. Although the Folkestone to Calais public ferry route operated throughout the war, passenger services from Newhaven ceased.

Newhaven was designated a military port and ferries were requisitioned by the authorities. Services were diverted to Folkestone

Newhaven Harbour.

SS Sussex.

to allow Newhaven to be used exclusively for supply troops on the Western Front. Newhaven Harbour station was closed to all but military traffic. Facilities at the port were improved with electric lighting and more railway sidings. The port operated for twenty-four-hours a day.

Although public ferry services ceased, the ships that plied the Sussex route were still involved in the action. On Friday 24 March 1916, the former Newhaven to Dieppe ferry, SS *Sussex,* was torpedoed in the channel whilst on a voyage from Folkestone to Dieppe. Two of its lifeboats capsized and over fifty people were drowned.

News of the attack quickly spread around the world. A correspondent to an Australian Newspaper *The Truth* said: 'This Queen of Trippers has found a glorious and tragic ending to a humdrum and peaceful career. In happier days she used to carry excursionists and happy schoolchildren across summer seas from Brighton to Eastbourne and back. What an end for her to be sunk somewhere off Zeebrugge in the horrid fog of a November night amid unfamiliar sounds of war. I confess that the end of this respectable old lady of the sea touches my imagination very vividly.'

Some of the passengers were Americans and the incident caused a diplomatic row between Berlin and Washington. President Woodrow Wilson addressed Congress a few days later giving Germany an

SUNK OFF BEACHY HEAD.

ANOTHER BRITISH STEAMER TORPEDOED.

Newspaper headline.

ultimatum to stop attacking passenger ships. Germany reluctantly agreed to the Sussex Pledge, promising that German submarines would no longer target passenger ships, and make safety provisions for passengers and crews before sinking merchant ships.

The pledge started from 4 May 1916 but on 16 January 1917 British code-breakers in Whitehall de-coded an intercepted telegram from the German foreign secretary Arthur Zimmermann to the German ambassador in Mexico. The telegram advised the ambassador that submarine warfare was going to resume on 1 February and urged Mexico to make war on the then-neutral US. As a result of this telegraph the USA declared war on Germany on 6 April 1917.

Another of the Newhaven to Dieppe ferries, the SS *Brighton* was used by President Woodrow Wilson when he sailed from Calais to Dover for a state visit to the UK on Boxing Day, 1918.

The port of Newhaven was used throughout the war mainly for the export of armaments and equipment to the Front. In 1916 a large number of army huts for use as canteens was exported through the port. Many of the extra dock workers, who had to be drafted in, were conscientious objectors.

The Newhaven to Dieppe ferry service was reinstated on Tuesday 15 July 1919.

CHAPTER 4

The Home Front

The prospect of invasion

In the Great War, the sights and sounds of warfare were ever-present in Eastbourne and Seaford. There were military camps that gave them the air of garrison towns. There were also the large grey dirigibles (airships) on constant patrol. Aircraft dropped bombs into the sea in the hunt for submarines, and the muffled booming of gunfire from sea battles was regularly heard by residents. In October 1914, an Eastbourne resident wrote to the War Office asking what preparations had been put in place for an invasion. The Under Secretary of State, Bertram Cubit, coolly replied, 'There is nothing in the present situation which would warrant the assumption that an invasion is probable or imminent. In the event of the enemy attempting to invade this country, instructions will be issued.'

During the Napoleonic Wars, 100 years earlier, locals feared a French invasion and in 1803 people living within 15 miles of the Sussex coast were instructed how to evacuate the area by wagon:

> *As soon as the alarm is given, pack your blankets and a change of cloathes* [sic] *for yourself and your children in the coverlid [coverlet] of your bed. Carry also what meal and meat and potatoes (not exceeding one peck) you may have in the house at the time, but on no account will any article of furniture of heavy baggage be allowed in carts. One hour only will be allowed for preparation.*

It is interesting to compare that to the notice given to the people of Seaford by Arthur Jack, of Seaford Council, under the Defence of the Realm Act of 1914:

> *Upon receiving notice to quit the district, all your household must take what food they can conveniently carry and proceed on foot by way of Blatchington Village over the Downs to Firle (all other roads will be stopped for military purposes). Any foodstuffs not removed must be destroyed before leaving and water taps left running. No wheeled transport, private or public will be available except for the sick and infirm as it will all be taken over by the Military Authority. Any bicycles in your possession must be removed or destroyed.*

At least in 1803 the evacuees were allowed carts.

One Seaford resident was not impressed with this approach – she was a single woman living with her maid and the two of them decided that if the town was invaded by the enemy they would stay put. She said, 'I had rather be shot on my own doorstep than be shot in the back running away to Firle.'

In January 1915 the mayors of Eastbourne, Brighton, Hastings and Hove decided that in case of an invasion a committee would be formed, led by the Duke of Norfolk, who was Lord Lieutenant of Sussex. Speaking on behalf of the south coast community, the Brighton mayor, Alderman Sir John Otter, issued instructions for the residents of all coastal towns under attack from the air or sea:

> *Inhabitants of houses should go to the cellars or lower rooms. If the house is on a sea-front, where it is exposed to direct fire from the sea, the inhabitants should leave by the back door and seek shelter elsewhere. Gathering into crowds or watching the bombardment from an exposed position may lead to unnecessary loss of life. If an aircraft is seen or heard overhead, crowds should disperse and all persons should if possible take shelter. Unexploded shells or bombs should not be touched as they may burst if moved.*

The role of the police

The role of the police changed dramatically once war had been declared. There was a lot of war work to do be done over and above normal policing, such as billeting duty, registering aliens, searching for spies and managing the blackouts. Until special constables were recruited, this extra work had to be done by fewer men. Twenty members of the Eastbourne Borough Force were reservists who enlisted. Regular police work was, in addition, made more difficult by the thousands of soldiers billeted in the area.

Edward Teale, Eastbourne's chief constable during the Great War.

But it was not only soldiers causing a problem, it was civilians too. In October 1914 a teenager, George Pascoe, was sentenced to six months imprisonment with hard labour for claiming to be an injured soldier of the Shropshire Light Infantry. He had bandaged his foot and claimed to have been wounded at Mons. In February 1915 George Wood, a lance corporal with the Manchester Regiment, was charged with stealing two bicycles. He was a journalist before he joined up and he offered, in his defence, that he could speak six languages. Presumably he hoped the authorities would see him as too useful to send to prison. He was bound over.

A great many special constables were employed and at the start of the war, before they were issued with uniforms, the only way to distinguish them was a striped arm-band worn on the left cuff. They were initially deployed at the waterworks to ensure there was no contamination of the town's water supply. The waterworks off Whitley Road was guarded twenty-four-hours a day until the end of the war. The army took over the duty early in 1915.

In April 1915, Leonard Dunning KPM, a former chief constable of the Liverpool City Police, visited the Eastbourne Borough Police and urged unmarried officers to join up. His speech was well-received as every unmarried officer and several of the young married ones immediately petitioned the watch committee to allow them to join the army.

Special constables.

Of the Eastbourne constables who did serve, one, PC Evenden, returned to Eastbourne a wounded hero in November 1914. While he was in the Coldstream Guards at the Front he was able to save the life of Lieutenant the Honourable Gerald Freeman-Thomas, who had also been wounded. The Lieutenant was the son of Lord Willingdon (governor of Bombay) and grandson of Earl Brassey, both local landowners. Evenden carried the wounded man to a haystack where his injured thigh was bound. The area had been captured by the Germans and Evenden stayed with his injured officer to make sure the Germans gave him hot coffee and food before Evenden made his escape. Unfortunately the officer died later that day. Lord Brassey sent the policeman a cheque for £10 by way of thanks for helping his grandson.

Because of the blackouts there were many more traffic accidents for the police to deal with. After a fatal accident in Eastbourne in May 1915, the coroner recommended that the corners and sides of main roads be whitewashed and in December 1915 the Eastbourne Borough

Application for Permit Book №. 189860

Issued at_ *Newhaven*

Style or Title } *Mr*
of Applicant }

SURNAME } *G E E R I N G*
(in capitals) }

Christian Names_ *David*

Permanent } *5 Tide mills Cottages*
Postal Address }
Bishopstone Nr Lewes

I hereby acknowledge the receipt of the above Permit Book and certify that I am a British Subject.

Signature of }
Applicant } *D Geering*

PERSONAL DESCRIPTION

Height_ *5* ft. *6* ins.

Sex_ *Male*

Build_ *Medium*

Hair, colour_ *Dark*

Eyes, colour_ *Grey*

Distinctive marks_ *None*

Entered by_ *PC Will*

Date_ *24/3/14*

PHOTOGRAPH
(to be affixed by the applicant, and stamped by Police).

This Form to be retained at the Police office which issues the Permit Book. [P.T.O.

Tide Mills pass.

Police were required to wear red lights on the front and back of their uniforms when they went out on night duty.

One of the duties of the police was to check identity cards. As well as the National Identity Card, issued from July 1915, there were local passes for those living within the restricted zone of the Tide Mills air station and permit slips to enter the camps.

Seaford Museum has a pass that allowed Mr C. Barrow to walk along the footpath between Seaford and Newhaven through the Tide Mills, but only during daylight hours. It is dated 2 April 1918 and is stamped 'Garrison Commander's Office – Newhaven'. Mr W. Green, a newsagent in Seaford, was issued with a pass to allow him to enter the military camps between the hours of Reveille and 7.30pm in order to sell newspapers and stationery. The typewritten note is Permanent Pass 784, which gives an indication of the number of passes issued.

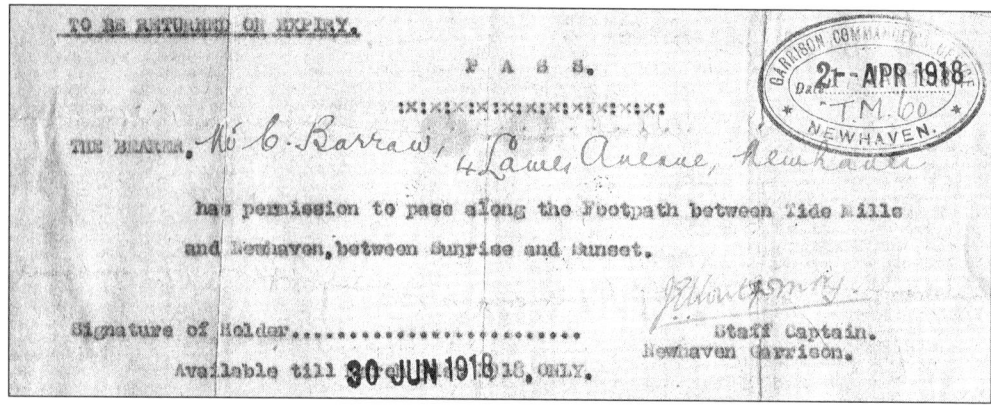

Aliens

In March 1916, Mrs Pauline Paget, the American wife of Almeric Paget, MP for Cambridge, was fined £3 at Eastbourne Magistrates Court for failing to notify the police that she had a French national in her house. The lady was a governess employed to care for the Pagets' children, Olive and Dorothy.

Karl Hemlar was an Austrian waiter and, although he was properly registered with the council as an alien, he was foolhardy enough to be found in possession of a loaded revolver. He appeared before Eastbourne magistrates in August 1914 when he was fined £100 with the alternative of three months' imprisonment.

Foreign nationals had to register their presence in a town. They also had to advise the police when they travelled. The same month, two German waiters, 20-year-old Frederick Woehrel and 25-year-old Karl Eldracher, left Eastbourne to work in Malvern. The Eastbourne Police issued permission and associated travel permits and advised them to report to the police when they arrived in Worcestershire. Because they failed to do so, the local magistrate sentenced them to four months imprisonment with hard labour, saying, 'Foreigners must understand that this order must be obeyed. If they did not choose to obey it they must take the consequences.'

On 9 September 1914, an Order in Council (legislation made by the Privy Council) detailed prohibited areas for foreign nationals. This included the coasts of Norfolk and Suffolk but surprisingly not Eastbourne.

Many German and Austrians failed to register with the police and, as reports from the Front started to filter through to England, the Home Office decided to act by asking police forces across the country to arrest enemy aliens who were of military age. As many as 400 were arrested in London alone.

In 1915, Alfred Roper, the headmaster of Ladycross School in Seaford, was fined £25 for failing to notify the police that he had employed a Dutch teacher. Mr Roper was outraged that his loyalty had been questioned, especially as his two sons were serving in the army. The case reached the ears of the Home Secretary, Sir John Simon, who told Parliament on 22 June that Mr Roper's loyalty and good faith were not in question, but it was necessary to enforce strictly the law in respect of aliens, particularly in sea-coast towns. He said there were insufficient grounds for interfering with the sentence. Even the headmaster of Eastbourne College was fined £1 for not registering two schoolboys from Siam (Thailand).

In July 1915 a German woman, Martina Lesbald, appeared before Eastbourne magistrates charged with failing to register. She told the bench that she understood that her son had arranged naturalisation for her in 1904, but he had been killed while fighting against the Germans in France in November the previous year. The case was dropped.

One German waiter who had been arrested in Eastbourne was William Bode. In April 1915, he was escorted from a detention ship moored in the Solent to get married at Ryde Baptist Church on the Isle of Wight. His best man was one of his armed guards.

But perhaps things were not always so difficult for aliens. On 30 March 1916, Viscount Templetown alleged in the House of Lords that 'a group of influential alien enemies were residing at Eastbourne in comfort and affluence'.

In March 1917, Parliament was told that a German woman, who had divorced her English husband, was running a boarding house in Eastbourne. Major Hunt, MP for Ludlow, said that she had relatives in the German army fighting against Britain and moreover her daughter Clara was employed as a censor with the British Ministry of Shipping. The Secretary to the Ministry of Shipping Control, Sir Leo Money, told the major that he had been misinformed. A lot of groundless scare stories were in circulation.

How many aliens were there in Eastbourne during the war? This question was asked in the House of Commons on 15 July 1918 by Colonel Richard Rawson, MP for Reigate. He wanted to know how many unnaturalized enemy aliens were residing in the prohibited area of Eastbourne and how many were living between Bexhill and Seaford. The Home Secretary, Sir George Cave, replied: 'The police registers show that eleven alien enemies resided in Eastbourne in 1915 and 1916, but they have been removed. There remains one alien whose nationality is doubtful, and as to whom it has been decided that he must be regarded as technically German and registered as such. No suspicion attaches to him, but steps are being taken to secure that he is employed on work of national importance outside the prohibited areas. As regards the second part of the question, there are three persons of enemy nationality residing in the coast districts mentioned, namely an invalid, a woman and a person who is believed to be technically a German but who is claimed as a Belgian by the Belgian authorities and has a son in the Belgian Army.'

Refugees and spies
Eastbourne and, to a lesser extent, Seaford became destinations for refugees, particularly Belgians. Families opened their houses to the 'poor Belgians', from the smallest terraced house to mansions like Little Hallands in Bishopstone. In March 1915, premises were opened in Eastbourne to enable Belgian refugees to set up businesses.

As the south coast was vulnerable to invasion, the seaside communities were particularly anxious about spies who were believed

Seaford schoolgirl, Connie Brewer, as "Poor Little Belgium".

to have infiltrated the population in order to prepare the way for an invading army.

The chairman of Eastbourne Borough Council reported to a meeting in August that spies had been seen making sketches at Jevington, Pevensey and between Seaford and Alfriston at High and Over. Charles Carter, the district surveyor, described an intriguing encounter. He said he had spotted a spy at Pevensey Sluice, near Norman's Bay station. He approached him and the spy dropped a map showing the coast from Eastbourne to Bexhill. Suspicious, Mr Carter followed the man to Eastbourne station and watched as he got on a train to London. He then walked up Grove Road to the police station where he made a report to a detective sergeant who, in turn, organized for the train to be met at Victoria where the spy would be arrested.

This makes an interesting story but does not really hold up to scrutiny. If the man was indeed a spy, he would have been unlikely to drop his map. The surveyor also seems to have had plenty of opportunity to challenge or even detain the suspect rather than allow him to make his way to London. And why walk all the way up to the police station at Grove Road to report the matter when he could have reported it to the Railway Police at Eastbourne station? They would have been in a position to alert the police at Lewes, who could then have stopped and searched the train. The Railway Police officer based at Eastbourne station was PC Sydney Poate.

Local boy scouts were briefed to play their part in looking out for suspicious characters. A few miles away in Rye, over-zealous boy scouts followed and detained two spies who turned out to be government inspectors testing the local telegraph wires. The girls at the Downs School in Seaford held a mock spy trial early in 1915. Their prisoner had been accused of spying for the Germans. The girls dressed up in wigs and gowns and listened to all the evidence, finding the defendant Not Guilty.

Speaking in May 1915, the author William Le Queux claimed that there were German spies of the Hanoverian Army Reserve operating throughout the south-east. He was, however, a known anti-German, having written a popular book *The Invasion of England 1910*.

Anyone with a German-sounding name was viewed with suspicion. In 1915 the Reverend Henry Von Essen Scott had to assure the people of Eastbourne that he had 'not a drop of German blood in his veins' after he received an anonymous letter telling him to get back to his own country. This must have been particularly distressing for him. He had previously served as chaplain to the Sussex Volunteer Corps.

In August 1915, Henry Noble was fined £3 by Eastbourne Magistrates for assaulting Kenneth Smith by punching him and tipping him over the railings on the seafront. In his defence Noble said that he thought Smith was a German. Even the royal family had to change its German name and on 17 July 1917 the House of Saxe-Coburg-Gotha became the House of Windsor.

The paranoia about spies was not entirely unfounded. In April 1915 a suspected German spy was arrested in Surrey and during the subsequent court case it was heard that he had spent two months staying at the Queen's Hotel in Eastbourne. A few months later in June a Scotsman giving his name as Irvine Graham was sentenced to three months imprisonment with hard labour after being found guilty of spying at Eastbourne.

The tourist trade
Seaford and, particularly, Eastbourne were towns that made substantial income from the tourist trade, though Seaford could never rival elegant

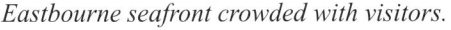

Eastbourne seafront crowded with visitors.

Eastbourne. Throughout the war they were determined that holidaymakers were not to be discouraged from visiting.

Eastbourne had five bandstands, the main one being on Grand Parade. In Seaford the single bandstand was on the seafront at the seaward end of West View. It was in place at the start of the war and had a similar birdcage design to the Eastbourne bandstands.

The bandstands were managed by the councils. In 1914 Seaford council handed over the running of the Seaford bandstand to a Mr R. Whiteread, but in Eastbourne the council continued to hold an interest. Eastbourne was determined to provide musical entertainment throughout the year and throughout the war. Although the municipal band had to be disbanded the council negotiated with the Devonshire Park Company to pay for two bands, one civilian and one military, to play throughout the year. There were over twenty players in each band and the council contributed nearly £4,000 towards the scheme. The bands were used to entertain visitors, and they were also a useful means to stir up national pride – and therefore an aid to recruiting.

Eastbourne's pleasure boats were able to operate throughout the war under licence from the council. The bathing machine industry found business more difficult as the beach defences made operation virtually impossible. In 1916, the council purchased the bathing machines in order to maintain them until the end of hostilities.

Yet the visitors still came. Over Easter 1915, over 1,000 visitors a day arrived at Eastbourne Station with twice as many at the weekends. Extra trains had to be provided, in spite of the poor weather. In 1916 Manuel II, the ex-king of Portugal, holidayed in Eastbourne for six weeks, giving organ recitals in local churches.

Eastbourne Pier remained open throughout the war and was especially popular with visiting soldiers. In the penny arcades the brightly coloured gaming machines operated by levers, triggers and buttons became increasingly war-like, with cowardly Huns as the targets to knock down. During 1915 alone, 500,000 soldiers were admitted free on to the pier and over 10,000 of them had attended entertainments at the pier theatre.

Hotels in Seaford and Eastbourne did a good trade, from tourists and the parents of boarding school pupils, and from families visiting soldiers at the camps. Hoteliers were briefed to look out for spies and breaches of the Registration Act. In January 1916 two pantomime girls

Eastbourne Pier.

were each fined £5 by Eastbourne Magistrates for staying in a hotel with military officers, posing as their wives and signing false names on their registration papers. There is no mention of any punishment for the two officers concerned.

The Grand Hotel

Eastbourne's Grand Hotel was one of the grandest hotels in the south of England. Built in 1876, it had over 200 rooms and was famed for its cuisine and its orchestra. The hotel continued to operate successfully throughout the hostilities, offering a high-status oasis for the wealthier war-weary. The headmaster of one local fee-paying school commented that upper crust parents stayed at the Grand, middle crust at the Hydro and lower crust at the Queen's. But it was all relative. Then, as now, many parents could not afford fee-paying schools at all.

The Grand Hotel's main problem was that it lost many of its staff – some enlisted, and some were Germans or Austrians. By 1916 the general manager, Ernest Page, decided to clear out most of the foreign staff, such was the strength of popular prejudice. Advertisements were endorsed 'No German, Austrian, Turk or Bulgarian (either naturalized

Grand Hotel, Eastbourne.

or non-naturalized) is employed in any capacity in this Hotel.' This made good commercial sense, although Mr Page later regretted the move as it caused hardship for the English wives and children of the men – and suitable English waiters were hard to find.

The hotel insured itself against damage by enemy action. By the end of the war 200 staff of the Grand Hotel had joined up and of these one in ten had been killed.

Lectures

To keep up morale in Eastbourne there were lectures by important and well-known speakers.

In March 1915 Lady Jellicoe (whose husband was to lead the British fleet at the Battle of Jutland the following year) begged people to send letters to men at the Front. She said that there were only four things a soldier on the front line thought about. Eating, sleeping, black marias (a nickname for German shells) and letters from home. A few weeks later, Sir Arthur Conan Doyle gave a spirited and optimistic talk: 'The Germans will now never make an advance along the Ypres line. The danger has entirely passed, for the line is impregnable.'

In April 1915 the Jam of Nawanagar gave a rousing speech. He was better known as the Sussex and England cricketer Prince Ranjitsinhji, who is still regarded as the greatest batsman of all time. As an honorary major he got close to the front line although, as an Indian prince, he was not allowed to get *too* close.

In May 1915 it was the turn of Sir Cecil Hertslet to give a lecture. He was consul-general in Belgium and had done much to evacuate refugees ahead of the German invasion.

Ranjitsinhji (playing cricket).

Pubs

In the days before radio and television the local pub was the usual source of evening entertainment. The licensing magistrates ensured that the strict new licensing regulations were enforced. The Defence of the Realm Act, which came into force on 8 August 1914, shortened pub opening hours to noon to 2.40pm and from 6.30pm to 9.30pm.

With many young men away women began to feel they could go into pubs that had previously been exclusively for men. The chairman of the Eastbourne Licensing Magistrates commented about the increase in the number of drunken women: 'It is disgraceful for women to drink when men are fighting at the Front.'

Schools

In the Second World War the schools were evacuated, but in the Great War they were not. The only exceptions were those in Seaford, which were requisitioned for war work. Ravenscroft School, for instance, was turned into a military hospital and the pupils moved to Eastbourne. Otherwise, the schools continued to function normally.

In October 1914, Eastbourne Education Committee decided that local schools must teach military drill as contained in the infantry drill book. This was a revival of a practice that had gone on in Eastbourne (and other) schools in the late-nineteenth century.

The children were kept up-to-date with war news and did what they could to contribute. Later in the war several schools undertook to send regular food-parcels to prisoners-of-war in Germany.

The old girls of Downs School kept in contact with their school and their exploits and news appeared in the school magazine. Their news changed dramatically after the war started and by 1915 their activities had turned overwhelmingly to war work. Many were nurses, some taught English to Belgian refugees, others provided food for local soldiers. Several adopted lonely soldiers and sent them regular letters and parcels. One, Miss Hughes, designed recruiting posters.

In 1890, the Reverend Edwin Leece Bourne, and known by everyone as ELB, was appointed headmaster of St Andrews School in Eastbourne. At the outbreak of the Great War many of his old boys enlisted. The first reports from the Front were optimistic. One lad wrote back to his former headmaster that he was looking forward to the next attack as it was 'going to be a really big show'. He said that he had the

St Andrews School, Eastbourne.

luck to be chosen to be up in the trenches and expected 'to get a splendid view of the whole thing'.

In December 1914, Bourne was quoting the Roman poet Horace: 'Dulce et decorum est pro patria mori' – 'How sweet and right it is to die for one's country.' But his tone changed during 1915 as the death toll of old boys steadily rose and war reports became less optimistic. By the summer of 1916, on average one old boy from the school was killed every week. No less than ninety-six St Andrews boys lost their lives in the Great War.

One old boy of the school was captured by the Germans and cheerfully wrote from his prisoner-of-war camp that it was 'just like being at school – only the terms are longer'. The boys were expected to work hard for the war effort. There was a coke shift, to collect coal from the railway station. Boys were encouraged to knit for the navy. ELB acquired wooden knitting needles and miles of dark brown wool, which his pupils made into scarves and gloves. During Easter term 1917, forty mufflers and twelve pairs of mittens were sent to the Royal Navy by the school. The boys were expected to clean windows, do gardening, and roll the school playing fields. They befriended injured soldiers and pushed them about in bath-chairs.

Schools in Seaford and Eastbourne lost many male staff to the war and women teachers were employed instead. Two of the St Andrews teachers, Bernard Harvey and Ronald Taylor, were killed in action. ELB preferred male teachers. He was forced to employ women to keep his school running during the war, but after the war he replaced them with men.

Rations for the children were sparse but the cooks tried to ensure there was meat on the table. The staff sometimes sacrificed their own rations to ensure the boys got a rounded diet. Stewed fruit and custard were regularly served for pudding. On Fridays, the leftovers were baked into what was known as resurrection pie. Surprisingly, there was no shortage of fruit and fruit drinks. Oranges were served for breakfast throughout the war, as was club jam. This was army issue plum and apple jam that was packed into a cylindrical cardboard tube with a tin cap at each end. Nor was there any shortage of lemonade, ginger beer, cherry cider and lime-fizz for the boys to drink after cricket.

The school holidays gave no respite for schoolchildren. When the girls of Queenswood School, Eastbourne, returned to school in 1917, they were asked what they had done for the war effort during the holiday. The responses included keeping chickens, gardening, fruit picking, hop picking, digging potatoes, working on farms, making jam, working in hospitals, making bandages, working in YMCA huts, packing parcels for prisoners-of-war and even doing clerical work for the government. Queenswood School assisted the war effort by knitting and the girls also made 200 bags for the Lady Smith-Dorrien Appeal. The girls raised over £500 for war funds by holding fetes and plays and also donating pocket money. They supported other organizations as well by running fetes and flag days.

The Smith-Dorrien Bag

The wife of the war hero Sir Horace Smith-Dorrien realized that servicemen often had nowhere to keep their personal effects after they had been wounded and were going through the hospital system. She designed a simple square bag that could easily travel with a wounded soldier on his trip home. Five million of these bags were made during the course of the war. The bags were 30cm by 10cm and made of unbleached calico with a white linen label and a drawstring. *The Times* of 26 March 1918 commented, 'Anyone who has seen the wounded arriving at Charing Cross must have noticed how the men cling to their little bag no matter how badly wounded they may be. Each contains a few things from which the fighting man will not be parted ... their pay-books, letters and other trifles.'

During a summer fete, girls from Eastbourne Municipal Secondary School had fun by bombing German cities. Squares were marked on a playing field with the names of the cities. Most points went to bombs that landed in the Berlin square.

The council and the community

The mayor of Eastbourne for 1916-17 was Alderman Charles Harding and in his end-of-year report he listed the war activities that had to be arranged by the council on top of its normal peace-time duties:

Arrangements for the storage of soldiers' furniture
The registration of war charities
War allowances to council employees
Payment to wives and dependants
Rent allowances for men on active service
Grants to the wives and dependants of those killed in action
Treatment, training and employment of disabled soldiers
Payment of separation allowances to dependants
Cultivation of war-time allotments
Enrolment of National Service Volunteers and their
   deployment
Granting of flying rights over the town
Enforcement of food orders
Allocation of retailers to householders
Paying bonuses to council employees for their war-work
Enforcing regulations regarding street collections
Controlling the supply of coal

At the beginning of the war there was some panic buying, but this fell away when it became clear that food supplies would remain steady. People were encouraged to grow their own food and keep poultry. In August 1917, Seaford Town's football pitch was ploughed over to grow crops. Immediately the war started the Duke of Devonshire, the main land-owner in Eastbourne, announced that he would forgo the rents to allotment holders in order to encourage as many people as possible to grow their own food. A weekly food control committee was established in Eastbourne in 1916 but there was also a food economy committee to co-ordinate rationing and the cultivation of food in allotments. The allotment scheme was not a success in Eastbourne. In the municipal year 1916-17, £218 was spent on planting potatoes but the value of the crop only amounted to £215. The total cost of the Eastbourne allotment scheme was £700 and a net loss was recorded.

In 1917 the government commandeered two-and-a-half-million acres of land nationally for farming, much of it worked by the Women's Land Army, whose numbers by that time had reached 250,000, many working on the farms around Seaford and Eastbourne. Farmers were often reluctant to have women working on their farms. A women's conference held in Eastbourne in July 1916 heard from Lady Wolseley that the difficulty was not recruiting women for farm work but getting male farmers to accept them.

Kate Rugg, Womans Land Army at East Dean.

At weekends, schoolboys worked on the farms. The boys of St Andrews School helped to pick the weed kilk (charlock) from fields planted with kale, always under the watchful eye of ELB. They sang school hymns and even nursery rhymes as work songs. Later in the war they were joined by German prisoners-of-war, who wore civilian clothes patched with red and yellow material to turn them into makeshift prison uniforms. The German prisoners sang along with the boys and would march back to their camps singing *Hickory Dickory Dock* in broken English, much to the consternation of their armed escorts.

Schoolchildren were used to eradicate cabbage white caterpillars from vegetables. This contribution to the war effort was considered to be fun and a welcome break from lessons. In the autumn, children collected chestnuts, which were sent to be used in the manufacture of nitro-glycerine. In August 1918, Seaford Urban District Council asked residents to collect fruit stones and nut shells, so that they could be baked to make the carbon for gas-masks. Apparently it took 200 peach stones to make the carbon for one gas mask.

The food control committee fixed the price of meat and other foodstuffs in order to discourage racketeering. During the war the price of most goods rose by 50 per cent but the price of meat doubled. The average consumption of meat dropped dramatically and food queues became the norm. The first commodity to be rationed was sugar, a large percentage of which had previously been imported from Germany. Cane sugar was imported from Britain's Caribbean colonies but the German U-boat threat disrupted supplies that had to cross the Atlantic. Ration books for sugar were first used in July 1917.

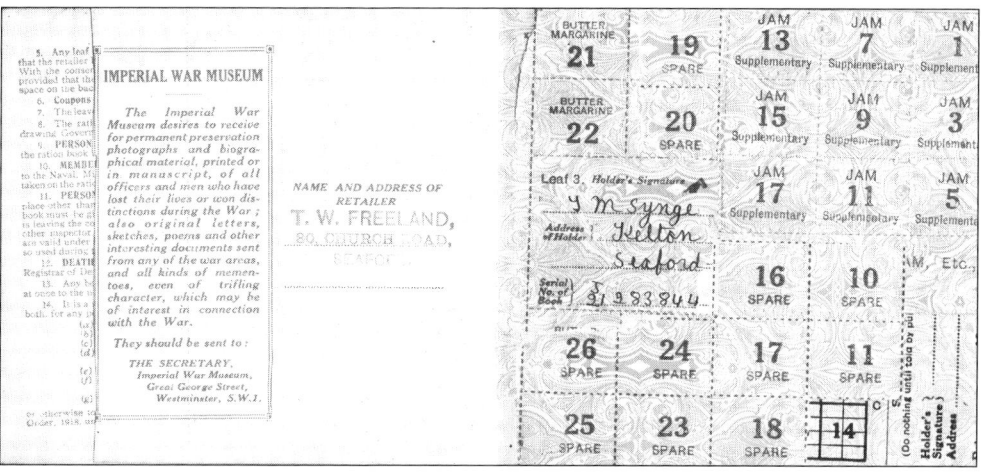

Ration books.

The council received complaints about the standard of food. In 1915 a local butcher was found not guilty of selling sausages containing a large percentage of bread. There were no regulations to prevent this. The Eastbourne committee received several loud complaints in 1917 that the rationing system favoured the rich, as working-class people did not have the time to stand around in queues. As a result, in February 1917 the council imposed conditions on shops as to the quantity of meat, butter and margarine that could be supplied. This scheme was based on the sugar rationing cards that had been issued. The mayor acknowledged that this was done without statutory authority but was necessary to maintain order. There were several prosecutions in Eastbourne for hoarding rationed foodstuffs.

Hardship at home
The Naval and Military War Pensions Act 1915 required local councils to establish committees to ensure that the pensions, allowances and grants made to families of men who had enlisted would not be affected by their military service. They also considered the care of the families of servicemen who had been injured in the war. The Eastbourne committee was chaired by the town clerk.

Shopping card.

Coal was one of the most vital commodities. It heated homes, offices and shops. It was also used for the manufacture of gas for lighting. Coal also powered the domestic electricity supply and water works.

The main port of entry for coal was Newhaven, which had been requisitioned for military purposes as soon as war was declared. The local gas companies and local councils petitioned for berths at Newhaven to be reserved for coal deliveries, but these requests were met with intransigence from the Admiralty. The Admiralty reluctantly agreed to make two berths available to colliers, but did not provide the necessary cranes and stevedores to unload them. To illustrate the effect of this, in December 1914 the collier *Harborne* from Sunderland took *two weeks* to unload rather than the usual two days. In spite of numerous requests, the Admiralty took no action.

The gas companies had to find alternative methods of getting coal into the area. Coal and coke were eventually brought in by rail from the South Eastern Railway's Thames-side docks at Erith, near Dartford in Kent. As a result of these problems, the cost of coal rose from 2s 11d to 4s 1d per ton in Eastbourne and from 2s 3d to 3s 5d in Seaford. This inevitably hit the consumers and in autumn 1915 the cost of electricity in Eastbourne rose from 5d a unit to 5½d a unit. A fuel and light committee was established in Eastbourne to control fuel sales

Coal was vital to keep the local schools running. Work parties of schoolboys collected it from the railway yards at the back of Eastbourne station and pulled it along the streets back to their schools with long tow ropes attached to hand-carts. They delivered to a number of girls' schools too.

The supply of coal continued to be a problem throughout the war In February 1919 the local MP Rupert Gwynne advised the House of Commons that the shortage of coal in Eastbourne and Hailsham was causing hardship to many local residents during the cold weather. He was assured by the president of the Board of Trade that steps would be taken to ensure further deliveries of coal.

Blackout

On 26 January 1915, Major Edward Teale, the chief constable of the Eastbourne Borough Police, issued an order that all lights in the town were to be extinguished between the hours of 5pm and 7.30am and that any person who failed to comply would be arrested.

Charged with breaching the lighting orders in May 1917, Emily Nichol of Hyde Gardens, Eastbourne apologized to the court. She had forgotten to draw her curtains at dusk. The case was dismissed. On a similar charge, the headmaster of St Andrew's School was fined 20 shillings. Throughout the war there were usually a dozen local people prosecuted each week for breaking the blackout regulations. Strict blackout regulations incidentally saved the council money on street lighting.

It was not just civilians who broke the regulations. The army openly flouted them. In March 1915, Seaford Council complained to the military authorities that the Seaford Camp was 'lit up like an exhibition'.

Bus and taxi services

Eastbourne bus services suffered from leakage of staff. By 1916, thirty-three men had gone and Mr Ellison, the general manager, was begging the Eastbourne Tribunal not to enlist any more of his staff. He was down to just seven drivers. The military representative queried whether a bus service was necessary. Ellison argued that in London, bus drivers were exempt from call-up and buses were used to convey (often wounded) soldiers. When asked why he did not employ women drivers he replied, 'If this course were taken, I would not like to be responsible for the safety of the public.' He later relented and allowed women to train as bus conductors, though he insisted they only worked on the newer vehicles as the older ones were prone to breakdown and women would be incapable of giving the driver a hand to fix them.

Another problem for Mr Ellison was that he had lost vehicles as well as men. At the beginning of the war, six new Leyland buses were commandeered by the army.

Buses and other vehicles were also taken from Chapman Brothers, a private charabanc and hackney carriage firm. In May 1915 a Private Ryan wrote to the local paper after being wounded at the Front at Ypres. During his evacuation he had been conveyed in a yellow painted Chapman's motor coach. These were known as the Eastbourne Canaries and later had canaries painted on the side.

The buses that remained in service continued to be popular. In June 1915 servicemen in uniform were allowed to travel on them for a flat rate of a penny. This caused an increase in passengers particularly boarding at the railway station, and this led to crowding. Permission to erect crowd barriers at Terminus Road was refused as was the request for a police point outside the station. As a result a bus inspector had to be on duty at the station from 11am to 9pm each day. This was no easy job, as the poor man was subjected to abuse and attack. He was kicked, punched in the face and pushed over. On one occasion in 1917 he was badly beaten by a group of soldiers who got away with the crime by giving the police false names.

Eastbourne's bus services ran throughout the war. A shortage of petrol required the buses to be converted to gas in order to maintain services. By 1918 the bus depot, now a munitions factory, had made 3,530 mines and over 370,000 Stokes Trench Howitzer Bombs. The Stokes Trench Howitzer was a 3-inch smooth-bore muzzle-loaded mortar bomb, first used at the Battle of Loos. The corporation made

Stokes trench mortar.

munitions to the value of £203,000 and this money was divided between the council and the workers.

During the war few taxis were motorized. Transport was still mainly horse-powered. In February 1916 a cab proprietor, Matthew Beeney, was sentenced to three months imprisonment with hard labour for accepting 80lb of oats (value 7s 6d) from two privates in the Hampshire Carabineers. The soldiers were brought before the court under armed guard and then handed over to the military to appear before a court-martial.

In 1917, a woman successfully applied for a licence to work as a taxi driver in Eastbourne. The local press were initially against her, citing the inability of women to carry heavy luggage.

Letters home

The postal service also continued through the war, operated by many temporary postal workers – both men and women.

Wartime letters and postcards were subject to strict censorship.

One of the first local casualties of the Great War was John Packett, who lived with his mother in Tideswell Road, Eastbourne. He was born in 1890 and joined the Royal Sussex Regiment in 1908 at the age of 18. In 1912 he became a railway porter at Eastbourne station, but when the war broke out he rejoined the army and was soon in France. He

Eastbourne post girls.

was wounded in the shoulder on the River Aisne, and came back to England to be treated at the military hospital in Woolwich. In September 1914 he wrote to his mother, 'Words fail me to describe the terrible battle last Monday. Hundreds of Germans are lying about dead and it is a wonder to me how I came out alive. I came over from France with about 220 other wounded and I didn't know a soul. I have only received two postcards from home since I have been away; they all went astray I suppose. It seems years since I went away.'

Such a letter would have been unlikely to get past the censors later in the war. Returning to the Front, John Packett was killed on 20 August 1916. He is buried in the London Cemetery at Longueval in France.

Early in the war the Brewer family, who lived in Claremont Road, Seaford, opened their doors for soldiers to be billeted. They received regular letters from the men and they make fascinating reading. In April 1918, Lance Corporal Whelan wrote from France complaining that he had not taken his boots off for ten days and that some of his men had had three hours sleep in seven days. He is, however, optimistic saying 'when the hun attack us he comes like a swarm of bees but is simply mown down like corn before a reaper'.

The Brewers' daughter, Connie, received a letter from Signaller Fred Sharpe from a convalescent camp in Le Havre, France. He had found her name and address written on an egg that she had donated to the war effort. He was also optimistic, ending the letter 'We are winning this war easy.'

Letters went in both directions and when Gunner Fleming of Western Road, Eastbourne received a letter at the Front telling him that his son was dangerously ill, he was granted four days leave to visit him. When he got home his son was out of danger and he returned to the trenches 'with much gratitude for the sympathy of the authorities'.

Wives and sweethearts

Too often the young men who enlisted paid the ultimate sacrifice. Then the emphasis was always on the loss suffered by their families, but many of the single soldiers had girlfriends who also experienced grief. To show that their menfolk were serving it became the custom for young women to wear sweetheart badges in the form of a regimental badge. They too, after all, were making a sacrifice.

The influx of soldiers into the town led to women forming liaisons with men from outside the area. In February 1916, Edith Maguire was sentenced to seven days imprisonment for harbouring a deserter, Private John Guy of the Loyal North Lancashire Regiment. Private Guy had been wounded and had surgery but Edith Maguire had hidden him when the detectives called. She lied to the police because she didn't want her boyfriend arrested. He was still ill. She had tried to urge him to return to his regiment but he had prevaricated.

Extra-marital liaisons like these often led to unwanted pregnancies. In May 1916 a scantily-clad new-born baby boy was left on the steps of the Leaf Hospital in Eastbourne. A note left with him by his mother asked for him to be properly clothed. Another young woman, made pregnant by a soldier at Summerdown Camp, try to commit suicide by drinking acid. She recovered in St Mary's Hospital, but was then sent to prison. Attempting suicide was a criminal offence.

Soldier sweethearts.

Private James Boyd of the Royal Irish Rifles married Kate Grenstead of Hastings at Eastbourne in 1915. Unfortunately for Kate her new husband was already married and he was arrested for bigamy.

Richard Thornton, mayor of Eastbourne 1911–12, returned home in 1915 after working for the Red Cross in France. He commented that the French government there did not allow fraternization. You never saw a soldier in France arm-in-arm with a local girl – unlike Eastbourne.

The liberated behaviour of soldiers and some civilians in wartime led to the opening in 1917 of a clinic for sexually transmitted diseases at the Esperance Hospital, Eastbourne. It was run by Dr James Adams of St Mary's Hospital until in 1919 the clinic moved to the town hall. There is a reference to a soldier being admitted to a venereal hospital at Seaford in December 1916. This is likely to have been a hut at the camp hospital.

In June 1918, an Eastbourne woman was convicted under Regulation 40D of the Defence of the Realm Act of having sex with a member of the armed forces while she was suffering from a sexually transmitted disease. The case was brought to the attention of the Home Secretary by Mr Lees-Smith MP, who complained that *her* name and address had been published whereas the name of the soldier had been discreetly withheld. He cited a number of convictions where women had been imprisoned for this offence even though no medical evidence had been offered to the courts. By the end of the war, 201 women had been prosecuted under the Act with one women receiving four months imprisonment with hard labour. This unpopular and unjust law was repealed in November 1918.

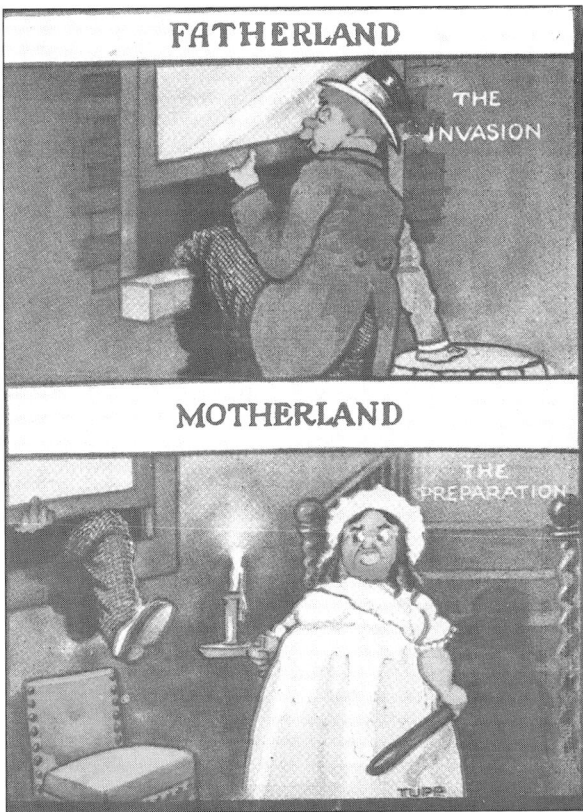

Invasion postcard.

CHAPTER 5

The Military Camps

Seaford camps

Seaford had been used by the military for training camps for many years. The Honourable Artillery Company held annual summer training camps in the town from the middle of the nineteenth century, the officers staying at the New Inn and the troops under canvas. The company held its exercises mainly on the open ground along the seafront, on Seaford Head and in the Cuckmere valley beyond. In a

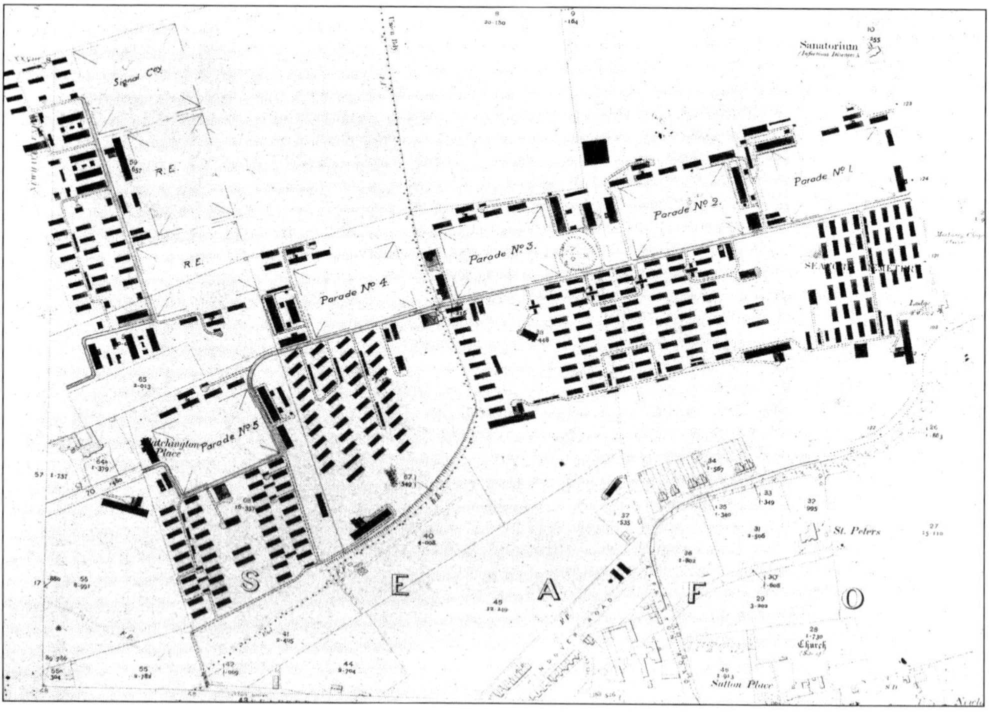

Plan of the North Camp, Seaford.

way this was the forerunner of the South Camp of the Great War. A second camp, Blatchington Camp, had its beginnings in the tented summer camps on open farmland between Blatchington village and Cradle Hill, land that is now covered with housing. Blatchington Camp began as a training camp for volunteers at the time of the Boer War. In 1914 the site became the North Camp.

Troops started to arrive in Seaford to train for fighting in France in September 1914. Writing later for a local magazine, one lady recalled the day the war arrived at her doorstep. It was 16 September. Her maid Hebe answered the door to find a burly policeman standing there. He asked how many men they could accommodate. The lady of the house pleaded that, as two single ladies lived in the house and they had only two beds, there was no room for any soldiers. The policeman's reply was, 'No question whether you will – only how many.' He toured the house, decided on three, and chalked '3' on the gatepost.

The soldiers billeted with this lady were probably from the 7th & 8th (Service) Battalions of the South Wales Borderers, who arrived in Seaford shortly after their formation in September 1914. They were billeted at St Leonards-on-Sea between December 1914 and May 1915. They returned to Seaford, but were in the town for only a couple of weeks before going to Aldershot for mobilization.

Another early regiment to arrive in Seaford was the 9th (Pioneer) Battalion North Staffordshire Regiment, who were formed a few weeks earlier and arrived in October 1914. As they were a pioneer (service) battalion, they were probably sent to assist with the construction of the camps. One of the men writing from Seaford at this time was a B. L. Lawrence. On 31 October he wrote to his friend Ogden from Seaford Camp saying that he would be in Seaford for many months. His fellow soldiers did not know how to form fours (drill), which was not surprising as there were only 100 rifles in the camp and no equipment. He believed there were 60,000 soldiers in Seaford, which was an exaggeration.

The people of Eastbourne and Seaford soon became accustomed to seeing columns of men marching around the town, often in civilian clothes. The 9th (Service) Battalion of the Kings Own Lancaster Regiment, raised at Lancaster in October 1914, were immediately transferred to Eastbourne for training. They moved between camps in Eastbourne and Seaford until the summer of 1915 when they moved

Naked Bathing Parade, Seaford.

to Aldershot prior to mobilization. A 1914 photograph shows several hundred men of the regiment marching along the Esplanade at Seaford for Bathing Parade, wearing civilian jackets and caps. The photo must have been taken in October or November, so the sea must have been cold.

The 12th (Service) Battalion of the Cheshire Regiment was raised in Chester in September 1914 and moved to Sussex, where they were billeted in Eastbourne and Seaford.

In the autumn of 1914 work began on clearing land for the South Camp, which was initially known as Chyngton Camp. It was sometimes referred to as Kitchener's Camp, but it was just *one* of a series of Kitchener's camps, which were laid out to a standard pattern using the 60-foot by 20-foot Armstrong army hut as the basic unit. The land belonged to Chyngton Farm to the east of the town, and was compulsorily requisitioned from the local farmer, Edward Gorringe, under the Defence of the Realm Act. Mr Gorringe was entitled to compensation for the loss of his living, but when he submitted a claim made out by a local valuer, it was rejected by the military who told him to apply for a much smaller amount. The case was taken up by local MP Rupert Gwynne, in spite of his political differences with the farmer, whom he described as a radical.

Initially the men were under canvas and the first hastily constructed huts went up on 11 November. The South Camp was designed to accommodate fifteen battalions. The large wooden Armstrong huts were built raised off the ground to deter rats, and they were heated by central stoves, which provided a focus for each dormitory hut and a place where soldiers could make tea and cocoa. The stoves caused problems. There were several outbreaks of fire. On 30 October 1914, several huts were burnt down at the South Camp. This was blamed on foreign-looking spies.

On 16 November 1914, George Terrell, MP for Chippenham, asked in the Commons when the camp would be completed and if troops would be occupying the huts before the camp was fully constructed. He was told by the Under-Secretary of State for War, Harold Tennant, that the huts would be completed shortly and that men would be moved into the camp as long as they did not impede the construction of new huts. Two days later, Lancashire MP George Haddock asked Tennant what steps were being taken to line the huts from the floor to a height of 4 feet to prevent the draughts that stopped the men from sleeping. The under-secretary replied that the first object was to build more huts that provided better cover than tents. When Mr Haddock said that some men from Seaford had complained that the huts were colder than the tents, the under-secretary dismissed the remark.

Kitchener's Camp, Seaford.

Seaford Camp under construction.

The following day there was another complaint about the running of the Seaford Camp. A number of veterans who had re-enlisted were training alongside recruits with no experience. Tennant said it was useful to have a number of old soldiers in each regiment during training. Many of them were experienced, though not fit to be sent to the Front. But they were carrying out important duties as policemen and cooks.

But the hastily constructed huts were not fit for purpose and on 2 December the South Camp was abandoned for repairs, which were to take until 4 March 1915 to complete. The troops returned to tents and many were billeted in private houses and hotels across the town.

The British and the Imperials
Regiments training at Seaford in 1916 included the 11th Reserve Battalion of the Gloucestershire Regiment, the 11th Reserve Battalion of the Loyal North Lancashire Regiment, the 15th Reserve Battalion of the Kings Royal Rifle Corps and the 14th and 15th Battalions of the Rifle Brigade. On 1 September they were amalgamated to form the 4th Training Reserve Brigade.

Training continued at Seaford until October 1916 when the 4th Training Reserve Brigade were relocated to Northampton to make way for Canadian troops. In October 1917 the London Command Depot at Seaford moved to Shoreham to make way for more Canadians.

At first the Canadians were billeted at the South Camp and British and Imperial troops at the North Camp. An incident in November 1917 changed this. Agnes Carter, a volunteer at the Rally Hut, reminiscing twelve years later, said 'a hot-headed Canadian Tommy, resenting the reprimand of an Imperial non-commissioned officer assaulted and injured him so severely that he died the following day. [Agnes Carter believed] that this was not allowed to get into the newspapers, but it was this unfortunate affair that finally decided the authorities to remove the Imperials to Shorncliffe [the barracks at Folkestone] and reserved both camps for the Canadians only.'

The North Camp may have been reserved mainly for Canadians, but other military units (and conscientious objectors) were also stationed there. In December 1917 the RAF were using the North Camp.

Summerdown Camp, Eastbourne.

Summerdown Camp, Eastbourne

Eastbourne's Summerdown Camp was established in 1914 for military personnel who had been wounded or otherwise injured. The camp was to the north of the workhouse (later St Mary's Hospital) on the East Dean Road. The first convalescents arrived in April 1915 and were issued with a blue uniform. This became a badge of honour in itself and the men were referred to as Blue Boys.

The Under-Secretary of State for War, Sir James

An Eastbourne Blue Boy.

Summerdown Camp, Eastbourne.

McPherson, was asked in the House of Commons about the facilities for wounded and legless soldiers at Summerdown Camp. He said, 'The camp is a little over 1½ miles from the sea, and the distance to shops in the Old Town is about 400 yards, and to the best shopping centre in Eastbourne about 1 mile. There are several routes from the camp to the sea, and on some of these there are seats. In Gildredge Park there are some 100 seats, the nearest being about 500 yards from the camp. There is also a good bus service from the centre of the town to within about 100 yards of the camp. There is only one legless soldier in the camp, and it is hoped to make arrangements to transfer him to a hospital nearer his home.'

In March 1916 two Victoria Cross holders, Lieutenants Handley Geary and Arthur Fleming-Sandes, appeared on stage together in the play *The Second in Command* at Summerdown Camp. Both had been awarded the VC a few months earlier, Geary at Hill 60 near Ypres and Fleming-Sandes at the infamous Hohenzollern Redoubt in France.

On Sunday afternoons, volunteers used Eastbourne buses to take injured soldiers for rides round the district. In 1916 buses were also used to take members of the Summerdown Camp band to the bandstand to give concerts. After about six months of this the council complained that the soldiers were being paid for playing and so should not expect free transport to their venue. It was also argued that playing music for money on the Sabbath was a contravention of the Sunday trading laws.

Kitchener's visit to Seaford

On Tuesday 20 July 1915, Lord Kitchener visited Seaford to review the troops, specifically the Ulster Division who were due to leave for the Front.

The review took place in the grounds of St Peter's School and surrounding land, south of the Alfriston Road. Thousands of people lined the streets and all the schoolchildren had been given time off to watch the parade.

A school magazine described the excitement of the day:

Lord Kitchener.

> *A wide stretch of undulating greensward. Suddenly the notes of a bugle-call thrill the air and die away across the meadow. In a moment the herbage becomes the rigid, khaki-clad ranks of a mass army. The air is full of intense, suppressed excitement. A number of Staff-Officers ride into an open space stretching along the southern side of the meadow and take their stand before the flag-staff and saluting base. The air resounds with the thud of horses' hoofs as officers gallop round the field.*
>
> *For a moment there is silence and then the sound of distant cheering is borne on the breeze. Another bugle rings out, and the air is full of the shouted commands of hundreds of officers. The swords of the Staff, and of a squadron of cavalry near them flash as they come to the salute. Away across the slope of the field, the sun glints on a rippling sea of steel as thousands of bayonets are presented in honour of the great Field-Marshal's arrival.*
>
> *As Lord Kitchener rides onto the field, the Union Jack floats out above him and the massed bands burst forth in loud and triumphant welcome. He rides around to inspect some of the units. Not a sound arises from the waiting host, rigid at attention, save for the pawing of a restless horse or the trample of those of the Staff as they accompany the Field-Marshal on his round.*

In a few minutes they return and group themselves round Lord Kitchener at his saluting-base. And then the marvel of the day begins. The troops start to march past in a never-ending stream – first cavalry, then battalion after battalion of infantry. Again and again the command "Eyes Right" rings out and again and again Lord Kitchener raises his hand to the salute in acknowledgement. For fully an hour the stream of men continues, rising as it were, out of the ground as they come up the far slope, down into the hollow and up again to pass the saluting-base. Nothing seems to escape Lord Kitchener as, laughing and chatting with the Staff, he indicates with a gesture qualities or failings – till the Red Cross wagons and the rear-guard of the Division have passed and he rides off the field, accompanied by the Staff.

Once more there is nothing but the wide stretch of green meadow-land, bordered by dark trees – quiet and peaceful where just before one of England's greatest soldiers has reviewed an Army.

The site of this grand parade is now a housing estate.

Life in the camps

The diaries of soldiers and the postcards they sent home show that life in the camps was often dull.

Some men whiled away the time writing. Lieutenant Arthur Baxter of the Canadian Engineers wrote a novel, *The Blower of Bubbles*, while he was in the North Camp at Seaford. He wrote at an improvised table near the hut-stove and he tried to ignore his fellow soldiers as they gathered each evening to drink cocoa and share titbits of food sent from home. If his hut-mates disturbed him, he threatened to read his novel out loud to them. Lieutenant Baxter went on to become the editor of the *Daily Express* in 1929.

There are glimpses into camp life at Seaford in the letters of B. L. Lawrence. The atmosphere in Seaford was 'rather too military' for him. As he was a subaltern (junior officer) he was saluted everywhere he went, and he had to respond to each salute, which made a walk into Seaford rather tedious. However he learned the art of the swank of being an officer. He was expected to be dressed to the nines at all times, never to acknowledge (except officially) the existence of an inferior rank and, when giving a command, to throw in as many 'damn's and 'bloody's' as possible.

Lawrence corresponded with Charles Kay Ogden, a linguist and philosopher. Ogden was the editor of the *Cambridge Review*. George Bernard Shaw and Thomas Hardy were contributors, as was Siegfried Sassoon the war-poet. The magazine was quite free-thinking, publishing several items that were critical of the war. As it reported on the plight of conscientious objectors, some even called it a pacifist magazine. Lawrence told Ogden that his copy of the magazine had been taken from his tent. 'When I later went in late for dinner, everyone was looking at me, and then I noticed at the head of the table of senior officers, the colonel with his head buried in the *Cambridge Magazine*. For one awful moment I thought that I should be cashiered but then his sense of humour came to the rescue and all passed off safely FOR THE MOMENT. I am, however, now viewed with suspicion as one of those extraordinary people who don't take the army seriously.' Even so, he asked Odgen to send down to Seaford more copies of the magazine.

Postcards were hastily produced by local printers, such as Wynter of Seaford. Most showed views of the camps but some featured patriotic rhymes with titles such as *Lord Kitchener's Boys at Seaford 1914*. Other postcards were less gung-ho and gave an insight into how unglamorous Seaford was. Verses include:

> There's only two lamps in the place, so tell to your mother
> The postman carries one and the policeman has the other
> And if you want a jolly night and do not care a jot
> You take a ride upon a car – only a

DOWN IN OUR Seaford Camp.

To be sung to the tune of "Back Home in Tennessee."

I'm so lonely, oh, so lonely,
    In our Seaford Camp,
Not worth a penny stamp
    I'm worse off than a tramp.
Father, Mother, Sister, Brother,
    All are waiting me,
I'm getting thinner, miss my dinner
    And my Sunday's tea.

CHORUS—

Down in our Seaford Camp,
    That's where we get the cramp,
Through sleeping in the damp,
    We're not allowed a lamp;
All we can hear there each day,
    Is " left, right," all the way ;
Sergeants calling, lance jacks bawling
    " Get out on parade."

We go to bed at night,
    You ought to see the sight,
The earwigs on the floors
    All night are forming fours.
If we're in bed in the morning
    You will hear the sergeant yawning
Show a leg there, show a leg there,
    Way down in our Seaford Camp.

Seaford Camp postcard.

car they haven't got
There are lots of little huts, all dotted here and there
For those who have to live inside, I have offered many a prayer
Inside the huts, there's RATS as big as a nanny goat
Last night a soldier saw one fitting on his overcoat.

The poem ends with the request that when, at the end of the war, the Kaiser is captured, he should not be shot but sent to Seaford to live among the rats – to see how long he lasts.

The post office at the North Camp was situated in the amenities hut and was established by Mr S. H. Everett, a London civil servant. The small post office kept letters until they were collected and on one occasion the Canadian Military Police arrested a soldier for stealing money from the letters of other men.

Outgoing mail had to be handed unsealed to a post office orderly, to be checked by a censor. For most Canadians, this was their first time away from home let alone in a different country, and the messages are full of wonder. They are also tinged with sadness. Private Eddie Henry of the 254th Battalion, Canadian Expeditionary Force, wrote home in August 1917 saying that Sussex was: 'very hilly and a splendid land for farming. The fields instead of having fences are bound in small green hedges, which present a picturesque sight and the oxen do farming over here in place of horses.'

Private Cameron Daubney of the same battalion thanked his mother for sending him butter: 'I had forgotten how good it tasted as we only get margarine here ... I have got used to being in the army and one gets hardened to almost anything. After you have been to France and seen your chum get killed or wounded alongside you, you think of it at the time but it is all forgotten in a day or two.'

The 254th Battalion had their own band, which sometimes played to entertain local residents. Corporal T. Simmons wrote in August 1917 that the band had been playing on Seaford beach but had been given notice that it was shortly to be sent to France to 'replace a band that had been wiped out'.

The soldiers were aware of the task ahead of them and seem to have been well-equipped and trained. One Canadian signaller reported that he had the latest equipment from the Front, but complained that during his training he had to write about 100 pages of notes a week.

The rally

Several huts in both camps were dedicated to the well-being and entertainment of the men. At the North Camp there were canteens provided by both the English and Canadian YMCA and a Catholic Recreation Room, but the favourite hut seems to have been the rally.

The rally was a large recreational hut established entirely by women from Seaford, many of whom had husbands serving at the front. Agnes Carter often worked there weekends and, as some of the women were nervous about walking alone through blacked-out streets, she escorted them home.

The head of the hut was a large woman who stepped in when things were getting out of hand. On one occasion she tackled two Canadians fighting with billiard cues, telling them in a loud but motherly voice, 'Get out, go home to your hut and go to bed.' Occasionally there would be a visit from members of the Canadian Military Police (CMP), identified by a red arm band.

Agnes worked on the till and helped soldiers who had difficulty in deciding between sausage roll or ham pie, penny cake or bun. Most of the men she served were Canadians but there were also a few Italians,

The Rally, Seaford.

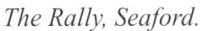

Americans and Scots, who were nicknamed Kilties. Some were 'huge magnificent men over 6 feet tall', whereas others appeared to be so young and delicate that she wondered how they ever passed their medical tests.

Agnes found that she was frequently called upon as a walking encyclopaedia. She helped with evening classes, accommodation for visitors and help in settling arguments, including the population of Australia and whether coffee grows on a tree or a bush. As this last question was to settle a wager for £2, she diplomatically said 'both'.

Camp food

Some Canadian soldiers found England expensive. Writing home in June 1917, Private Garnet Dobbs of the 6th Battalion Canadian Expeditionary Force complained, 'It costs a shilling (24 cents) for as much candy as you can buy at home for a nickel. A little box of matches is 10 cents. Little biscuits like ginger snaps and arrowroots are three biscuits for 3 cents and almost all eatables are correspondingly high. You can't get white bread at all – they use a sort of rye bread and sugar is also scarce.'

The Canadian soldiers were not impressed with the quality of the food. One described English food as 'punk'. Writing in November 1917, Private John Cushnie reported home that the camp canteen had just started serving mashed potato instead of boiled. 'We had three pretty fair meals today, which made up for the rotten meals of fish yesterday. For dinner we had roast heart, mashed potatoes, carrots, apple pudding, bread and margarine.'

The camps were well-stocked with beer supplied by Robin's Brewery in the High Street. In February 1915, Company Sergeant Major Reynolds of the Loyal North Lancashire Regiment was found guilty of embezzling over £28 from the Regimental Sergeants' Mess that was due to be paid to the brewery. He was sentenced to six months imprisonment with hard labour.

Sport

Sport was a popular way to pass the time in the camps. It also helped to keep men fit and engendered a spirit of camaraderie.

One man who significantly changed the face of sport in the camps was the eccentric William Grantham, who held the rank of honorary major. He lived at Blaneath Manor at Chailey and was often seen wearing a traditional Sussex smock and a tall top-hat made of beaver-skin. During the Great War he was the major for the 6th (Cyclist) Battalion of the Royal Sussex Regiment but did not see action. He was the military representative at the East Sussex Military Appeal Tribunal and the Sussex representative on the National Military Tribunal. His son (also William) joined the Royal Sussex Regiment in 1915. But after the young man was injured his father set about introducing the game of stoolball.

Stoolball had been played in Sussex for centuries. It was an unusual game as it could be played by all – young or old, men or women and even those with a disability. Major Grantham thought this an ideal game for injured servicemen. Even nurses could take part. The game was taken up at local military hospitals. In October 1917, Major Grantham arranged an exhibition match in Eastbourne that had to be abandoned temporarily. The soldiers hit the ball so hard they split three of the bats.

Stoolball is similar to cricket but the wicket is a wooden board at shoulder height. The bat is a rounded piece of wood about the size of a man's hand. After the war Major Grantham toured the world promoting the game and matches were arranged in Iceland, Tokyo, Beijing and Moscow. Stoolball is still played regularly around Eastbourne, and Seaford holds an annual tournament in the Salts.

As there were many Canadians billeted locally, particularly at All Saints Hospital at Meads, baseball was regularly played by the men both in Eastbourne and Seaford. Local schools hosted these games although one headmaster commented loftily that 'baseball as a sporting game leaves much to be desired'. Other games played by the Canadians in Seaford included lacrosse and push-ball – a team game played with a giant ball 6 feet across. After one winter game of rugby a Canadian complained that the Sussex mud coated the players from head to foot, was sticky and hard to get off.

Being by the sea, bathing was also an option. Photographs show hundreds of men swimming naked in the sea between the Martello and Seaford Head.

A boxing ring was erected at the North Camp taking advantage of an old chalk pit to make a natural arena. Tiered benches were constructed but seating for popular matches was supplemented by seats brought from the surrounding huts and even the local schools, so that up to 6,000 spectators could watch.

Friday, 1 June 1917 saw a grand boxing tournament at the North Camp. It had been arranged for the London Command Depot under the patronage of Lord Glanusk (Colonel Wilfred Bailey CB, DSO) of the Grenadier Guards. The band of the Dragoon Guards provided musical entertainment between bouts.

This was to be a major event and the referees were Arthur Bettinson and Eugene Corri of the National Sporting Council. Bettinson was a former British Lightweight Champion, who had founded the NSC in 1891. He standardized weight divisions and arranged for the

Boxing at Seaford.

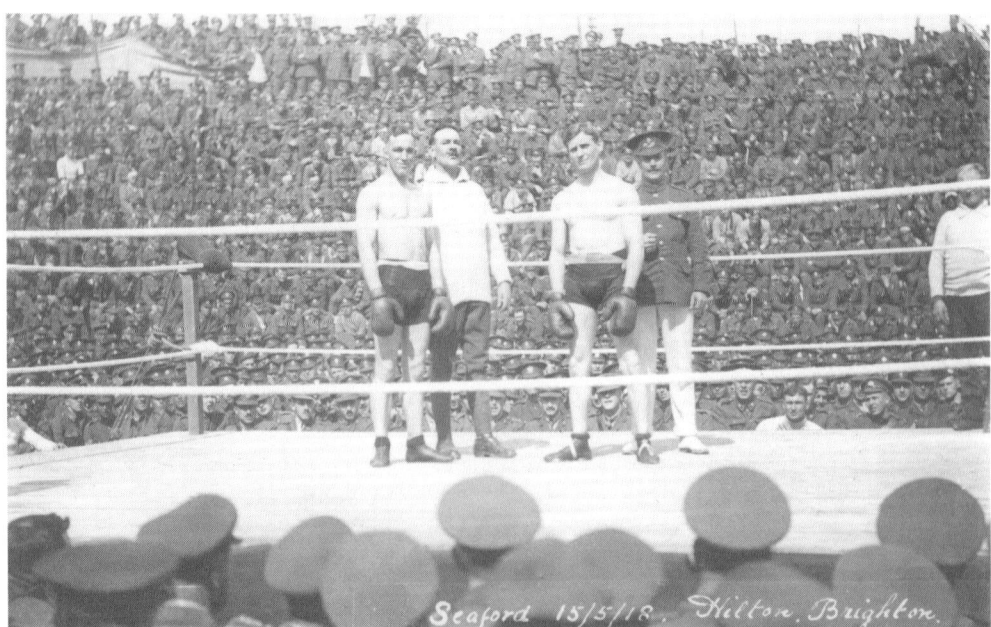

presentation of championship belts donated by the first NSC president, Lord Lonsdale. Corri was an internationally famous referee.

After the band of the Dragoon Guards played, the boxing started with some preliminary rounds followed by a ten-round contest between Staff Sergeant Zimmer and Harry Jones of the Royal Fusiliers. Zimmer was one of the instructors at the camp and was able to beat Jones on points.

The star event was a match between two champions, Frank Slavin (billed as the ex-heavyweight champion of the world) and Ernest Chandler (who at that time was the serving heavyweight champion of the world). Prior to the match, Major James Fowles told the assembled crowd how honoured he was to present the two men, especially 'Paddy' Slavin who twenty-five years previously, almost to the day, had fought Peter Jackson in one of the most celebrated fights of the Victorian era. He said that Slavin had not put on gloves since 1892, but had decided to fight for the sake of old friends. This was untrue, as records show that Slavin had taken part in at least twenty-seven fights since that date. Slavin became champion of New Zealand in 1888 and his most famous match had been the one with the black boxer Peter Jackson for a purse of £2,000.

Chandler, at 26, was at the height of his boxing career. He was amateur heavyweight boxing champion of the world. Not surprisingly, at the North Camp boxing match he beat Slavin in just three rounds.

Entertainment

In December 1917, the RAF built a temporary theatre for Christmas entertainment in Seaford. It was called the Pontodrome. This theatre was constructed under the direction of Flight Sergeant Morley and the stage manager was Air Mechanic (3rd Class) Harold Albert Burdick. In civilian life, Burdick was a theatrical agent. He was responsible for putting together the evening's programme of entertainment, and he also played several parts in the revue, including a policeman and a jilted husband.

The camp magazines give an insight into military camp gossip of the day. *The London Command Depot Magazine* of June 1917 tried to embarrass a member of the company with the barbed comment, 'A married soldier of 3 Company thinks he is single by the seaside.' And a London Scottish soldier was suspected of *train-spotting* at Seaford station.

Soldiers in trouble

Just a week after war was declared, on 13 August, two soldiers, Private Stanley Bennett and Bugler Herbert Foster of the Royal Fusiliers, were drowned in the sea at Eastbourne while staying at a cadet camp. Theirs may be the first military deaths of the Great War in this area, though their names do not appear on the Commonwealth War Grave Commission roll of honour. In December 1914, John Mainwaring of the Lancashire Fusiliers fell down some stairs whilst training in Eastbourne and died a few hours later. His last words were 'Eight thousand Germans'.

One year later, Private Marshall of the Royal Army Medical Corps was killed when he went to the assistance of people involved in a car crash in Seaside, Eastbourne. The car containing a nurse and three children had collided with a roadside street lamp electricity cabinet. When he went to help he touched some cables and was electrocuted. 'As if struck by lightning', he was instantly killed.

There were also, inevitably, crimes and misdemeanours. In January 1916, Lieutenant Arthur Hurry of the Gloucestershire Regiment was fined £4 with 2 guineas costs for avoiding paying his railway fare between Lewes and Eastbourne and for giving, when challenged, a fellow officer's name as his own. In May 1916 Lieutenant Taylor of the Royal Flying Corps was heavily fined – £12 – for dangerous driving along Eastbourne seafront. A young lady was nuzzled up to the airman, who was driving at over 45 mph. Taylor was clearly on a spree and not on official business. The case of Lance Corporal Homersham, who appeared at Eastbourne Magistrates charged with speeding on his motorcycle in November 1914, was very different. His lieutenant appeared in court on his behalf to give evidence that Homersham had been carrying urgent despatches between Lewes and Bexhill. He had been instructed to go at great speed. Naturally he was acquitted.

A strange incident occurred in March 1916 when 28-year-old Rifleman 4446 John Hemstock was found at the bottom of a 35-foot dry well in Eastbourne. How he managed to be there is not recorded and he himself was unable to give an account of his adventure. He managed to survive the ordeal despite having no food for eight days. He was killed in action in northern France four months later.

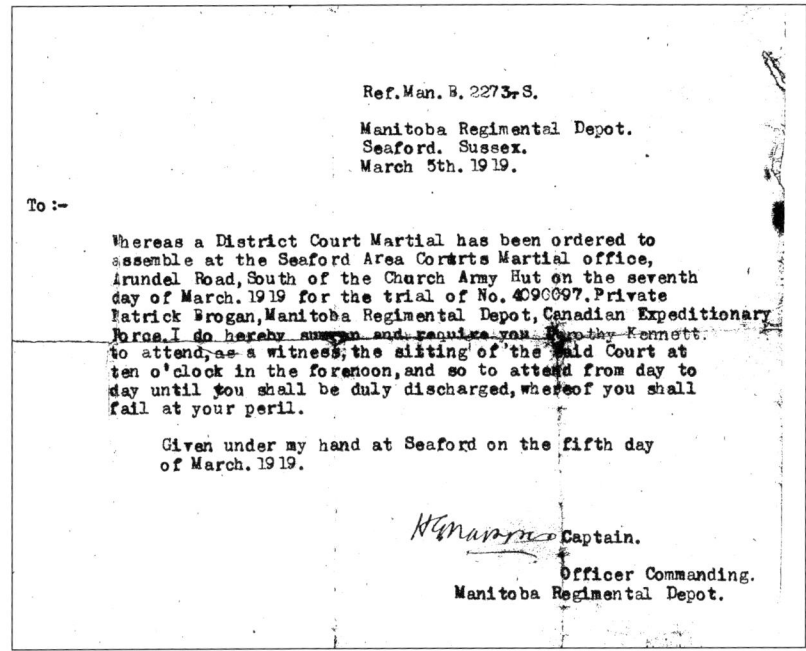

Court martial paper.

Courts martial

A Court Martial Office existed in Arundel Road in Seaford and was described as being 'just south of the Church Army Hut'. Details of courts martial for serving soldiers are scant; there is one surviving reference, and that is very incomplete.

On 7 March 1919, a Canadian soldier, Private Patrick Brogan of the Manitoba Regiment, appeared before the court martial at Seaford. Brogan was an Irish steelworker who had been drafted into the Canadian Army in January 1918. Neither his crime nor his punishment are known. All that is known is that one of the witnesses called was a local Seaford woman, Dorothy Kennett.

CHAPTER 6

Men of the Empire

The Irish

The first of the Empire troops to arrive in Seaford were the newly raised 36th (Ulster) Division. They arrived in Seaford in July 1915 after travelling by train from Belfast to Dublin, the ferry to Holyhead and then by train again via Crewe to Seaford. The political situation in Ireland at that time was fragile and most of the men had been recruited from the Ulster Volunteer Force. They were already trained as a military force, which made a huge difference to the impression they made at the Seaford Camps.

On 12 July, soon after they arrived in Sussex, the Ulstermen celebrated Orange Day. Seaford residents noticed that many of the troops walking around were wearing orange sashes and decorations, and by the evening a parade had been arranged with bands, banners and flags. Many local people turned up to watch what must have been a unique Orange Day Parade, one of the few to be held on English soil. There have been some Orange Parades in the north-west, but few can have been attended by so many Ulstermen. At 6.30pm men gathered at the YMCA hut in Arundel Road, many of them wearing the insignia of the Loyal Orange Institution of Ireland. At the hut there were rousing loyalist speeches. The chairman of the meeting boldly predicted that by the next Orange Day (in other words by 12 July 1916) the Germans would have been defeated, the war would be over and the men would all be home on Irish soil.

When Lord Kitchener came to Seaford to inspect the troops on 20 July he told Major-General Powell that he was relieved to see a division ready for the Front at a moment's notice. In the same spirit, Kitchener later told Sir Edward Carson, the Unionist leader, that the 36th Ulsters were the finest division in his new army.

Many of the Ulstermen were visiting England for the first time and they seemed to enjoy their stay in summer Seaford. They described how, when high up on the Downs, they could hear the guns of France. They attended church services at St Leonard's. On one occasion the vicar, seeing his pews full of troops, decided not to ask for a collection. At the end of the service the offertory box was so stuffed with coins that it fell off the wall and broke.

Ulster Crest. (permission granted to use)

Practice trenches were routinely cut into the chalk above Seaford, but on one occasion a trench was cut across one of the gallops of an Alfriston training stable. An apologetic letter was sent to the stable owner who replied that he was happy that his land was being put to good use and offered his gallops to the young officers for training purposes.

Three soldiers of the Ulster Division died while in Seaford. Two died in one incident. One was 36-year-old Thomas Pollock of Dromore, County Down, who was accidentally drowned on 18 July 1915 while trying to rescue 19-year-old Driver Robert Wilson of the Royal Army Service Corps, attached to the Ulster Division. The two were swimming near the Buckle Inn when Wilson got into difficulties. The undertow pulled him away from the beach. Pollock, a married man with several children, tried to rescue his comrade but he too was drowned. Thomas Pollock's brother Archibald was also training at the North Camp at the time. The funeral, with full military honours, was the first of many to take place at Seaford Cemetery and it aroused a lot of local interest and sympathy.

Irish grave.

The funeral party met at the North Camp (Blatchington entrance) where over 300 men of the Army Service Corps stood in silence. The funeral procession was led by fifteen men of the Royal Irish Rifles marching slowly with their guns reversed. Next were the bands of the Royal Irish Rifles and Royal Inniskilling Fusiliers, over sixty men in all. Each of the drums of the band was muted with black cloth. Next came two horse-drawn carriages carrying the union-flag-draped coffins of the men. Their caps, belts and guns had been placed on top, and the carriages were awash with colourful wreaths. On either side of the carriages the pallbearers marched and behind them were members of the families of the men. Following this were the two horses usually ridden by the soldiers, the men's jackboots had been reversed in the stirrups. The funeral proceeded along Claremont Road, Clinton Place and Sutton Park Road to the cemetery where, as the coffins were lowered into the graves, the firing party fired three volleys over the graves and the last post was sounded.

Similar military funerals were held at the Ocklynge Cemetery in Eastbourne.

There was also at least one Irish wedding. Corporal Gordon of the Royal Irish Rifles married Mary Adair at the Congregational Church in Clinton Place. Mary was not a local girl. She had travelled from Winnipeg in Canada for the ceremony. Corporal Gordon was given a few days' leave and he took his new bride away for a honeymoon in Glasgow.

West Indians

Early in the war, men from the Caribbean travelled to London to enlist in the army. Some were so keen to enlist that they stowed away on board ships bound for England. In May 1915, nine men from Barbados appeared in court in East London after they had been found on board a steam packet that had arrived at the nearby docks. The men were taken to the nearest army recruiting office but were turned away on account of their colour. Their treatment caused friction between the Colonial Office and the War Office and after an intervention from King George V permission was granted on 19 May 1915 for a West Indian contingent to be recognized. The War Office was obviously not prepared for the support and enthusiasm from the men of the West Indies. Private Griffiths, who trained at Seaford Camp, was from

Trinidad. He said, 'Everything I know has been taught to me by the English and when I heard Lord Kitchener's appeal for men I could not help but come.'

A West India Contingent Committee was established in London and their office became a place where West Indians arriving in London to join up could get advice. It was decided that black volunteers should be sent to Seaford to await a decision on their recruitment and deployment. The first contingent of West Indians, mainly from Barbados and British Guiana, arrived in Seaford on 5 September 1915. A month later a western port saw the arrival of 750 more men from the West Indies. Later on their day of arrival, a frosty 4 October, they marched from Seaford railway station along Blatchington Road and up Blatchington Hill to the North Camp. The western entrances to the North Camp were 200m along Homefield Road and Upper Belgrave Road. North Camp Lane was one of the entrances.

The British West Indies Regiment was established on 26 October and Army Order 4 of 1916 (passed 3 November 1915) conceded that the regiment should be recognized as a corps for the purposes of the Army Act.

On 25 November 1915, trains containing another 725 black recruits arrived at Seaford station and, marching up to the North Camp, they joined the four companies already established there:

A Company – British Guiana
B Company – Trinidad
C Company – Trinidad and St Vincent
D Company – Grenada and Barbados

West Indian regimental badge.

Later drafts were formed into E Company. The different companies had identification marks. One was a swastika, an ancient Hindu symbol of auspiciousness.

One of the first duties the men carried out was attending the funeral of Corporal James Lawrence Brown of St Vincent. He was accidentally killed on 21 November when he came off his bicycle after it careered down Exceat Hill. He lost control and his head struck a tree.

In November 1915, a ladies committee was established in London chaired by the Countess of Stamford. The committee set about improving the life of men at the Seaford camps and supplying much-needed warm clothing as well as cigars and cigarettes. The committee also arranged a flag day across the Caribbean islands. The money was used to provide the men with parcels, which contained handkerchiefs, soap, boots, badges, clothing, writing materials, shaving equipment, games, fruit, wallets, books and magazines.

In November 1915, a group of black soldiers marched in the Lord Mayor's Parade in London. The *Daily News* called them 'huge and mighty men of valour'.

Martha Grey, Countess of Stamford.

As well as troops from the colonies, German prisoners-of-war and captured guns were paraded at the 1915 Lord Mayor's Show. The parade, to introduce the new Lord Mayor of London, has taken place annually, in peacetime and war alike, since 1852. The 1915 parade was timed to coincide with ten recruitment meetings and as the parade passed the recruiting offices more and more men joined the parade.

Although seeing non-white faces in Seaford was unusual it was not unknown. The town was a port in medieval times and close to the later port of Newhaven, so Seafordians would have seen many visitors from overseas. In 1683 two black people were married at St Leonard's Church and in 1822 the local freemasons had a black member. There would, inevitably, have been elements of racism and discrimination, but the black regiments' stay in Seaford was accepted by local residents. The soldiers were known affectionately as Westies. The men were smarter than the average white soldier, wearing white shirts and black ties when off-duty, and some Seaford residents at first imagined they must all be padres. Quite a number were well-educated and accustomed to English ways, so they soon got to know some of the local people and many made friends. The vicar of St Leonard's at the time later wrote, with some condescension, that the men of the British West Indies Regiment were 'at least equal with most of the white regiments of which we have had experience'.

In December 1915, the *Eastbourne Chronicle* reported: 'At the outset, local people were inclined, not unnaturally, to be sceptical at the arrival of these strange soldiers of the king, and therefore the tribute of praise is all the more sincere when, after a couple of months' experience, the residents generally speak in high terms of the behaviour of these men. Their presence is a striking tribute to the strength of the British Empire.' That month fifty-three West Indian soldiers joined local people to be confirmed by the Bishop of Lewes. *The Chronicle* reported that it was 'inspiring to see the reverent attitude of the soldiers who, being 4,000 miles from home, discharge their duty to the Empire and found a warm welcome in their mother church'.

The Seaford branch of the Ancient Order of Foresters, which had many members serving in the armed forces, discovered that several of the West Indian soldiers at the North Camp were members of their own

West Indians at Seaford.

organization. They were duly invited to attend local meetings. During one of these, Private Clement of the Pride of Hope Court of the Foresters of Trinidad said, 'We have left our homes and comforts because the call-to-arms is as much to us as it is to an Englishman. We are all British and are proud to be members of the Empire and we will shed our last drop of blood to uphold its integrity.'

Not everyone in Seaford was so accommodating. In October 1915, Lawrence Graham appeared at Lewes Magistrates charged with disaffection for making remarks likely to jeopardize recruiting to His Majesty's Forces. Graham had accosted black soldiers, telling them that white men should be left to fight their own battles: 'West Indians are fools for fighting for the Empire. Why don't you lay down your arms and do no fighting?' In the bar of a Seaford hotel he asked two black soldiers why they had enlisted on such little pay when Churchill, Asquith and Lloyd-George were being paid £15,000 a year. For his subversion Graham was sentenced to six years' imprisonment with hard labour.

Further evidence of the acceptance of the men locally is shown by the visit, in December 1915, of two headmasters from schools in Trinidad and British Guiana to Church Street School Seaford. There is also a remarkable letter that has survived. Private 875 Eric Hughes of the British West Indies Regiment wrote to two Seaford girls, Dorothy and Doris. He had evidently met the girls before as he sent his regards to their mother, then he asked the girls if they would accompany him to the cinema on Thursday night. We have no way of knowing whether Eric got his double date but it says much for race relations at the time that he had the confidence to ask.

Coming from a Caribbean climate to wintry Seaford was a massive shock to most of the men. Many of the West Indians succumbed to mumps and pneumonia and, between October 1915 and January 1916, nineteen of them died. Their Commonwealth War Graves can still be seen at Alfriston Road Cemetery, Seaford. By the end of the war the British West Indies Regiment would have lost 178 men to enemy action – but over 1,000 to infection and illness. In April 1916, the British West Indies Regiment went to Egypt. On their departure the future prime minister, Andrew Bonar-Law (who was Canadian by birth) wrote to Colonel Blanchard:

On the eve of the departure of the British West Indies Regiment to serve abroad, I desire, as Secretary of State for the Colonies, to express to you and through you to your Officers, Non-Commissioned Officers, and Men of the Regiment my warmest good wishes for you and their welfare and success in the tasks that lay before them. I only regret that circumstances prevent me personally delivering the message to them.

The ladies committee petitioned for equality of pay for the British West Indies Regiment. The army had designated the regiment as a native unit and until Army Order 1918 they were paid less than regular (in other words, *white*) troops. The difference in pay was not based on the fact that black soldiers came from the colonies. White soldiers recruited in South Africa were not subject to this discrimination.

Canadians
The Canadian soldiers were the main occupants of the Seaford Camps from 1916 until the end of the war – and for several years afterwards. Much has been written about the Canadians in Sussex. They were stationed throughout the county in both World Wars.

It would be no exaggeration to say that during the war hundreds of thousands of Canadian soldiers passed through this area of Sussex, and the scale of their sacrifice is plainly seen at Seaford Cemetery where nearly 200 are buried.

Early military graves at Seaford Cemetery.

Responsibility for the Seaford Camps fell to Lieutenant-Colonel Stanley Douglas Gardner MC, who was in charge of both North and South Camps for three periods: from 21 October 1916 until 22 August 1917 from 22 September 1917 until 13 June 1918; and from 28 June to 18 July 1918. Gardner, born in London in 1880, was an accountant in civilian life though prior to the war he had joined the London Regiment. In 1914 he was living in Canada where he joined the Canadian Expeditionary Force as a captain in September 1914. He was wounded in France and invalided to England where he later took his post in Seaford. Just a month after leaving Sussex in 1918, he was back in France as commanding officer of the 38th Battalion of the Canadian army. He was wounded again on 28 September and died two days later. He is buried at Duisans British Cemetery near Arras.

The 10th Canadian Stationary Hospital arrived at Seaford by train from Shorncliffe Barracks in Kent on 2 November 1916. The men marched to the South Camp and were attached to 103rd Battalion Canadian Expeditionary Force. All aspects of a soldier's health were considered and towards the end of the war the Canadian Army Dentistry Corps had a hut at the South Camp. The corps consisted of twenty-four officers and eighty-four other ranks and also had responsibility for Canadian soldiers across Sussex.

Canadian badge at North Camp.

Canadian Engineers' Orderly Room, Seaford. Design 40ft long 10ft wide by Spr. Stenhouse.   Miller Brighton.

On 5 November 1916, Ravenscroft School on the junction of Sutton Avenue and the Eastbourne Road was taken over as a Canadian hospital, after being occupied by the Royal Army Medical Corps for the previous two years. The buildings could accommodate 100 men and were staffed by nurses from the Canadian Red Cross.

Dr George Bowler, who was 51 years old, was the mayor of Kitchener, Ontario. His home town had previously been called Berlin, but the name was changed to Kitchener when war broke out. Bowler joined the army as a major in 1915. Eighteen months later he was Deputy Assistant Director of Supplies for the Canadian Army Medical Corps in Sussex, but by late October 1916 he was complaining about severe headaches and on 10 November he was seen to fall from the cliffs at Seaford Head and was found dead on the beach below.

In January 1917, the 10th Canadian Hospital took over All Saints Convalescent Hospital in Eastbourne. By the time the two hospitals, one in Seaford the other in Eastbourne, were decommissioned in April 1919, they had treated over 16,000 patients.

On 22 July 1917, the Canadian Signalling School moved to the North Camp in Seaford occupying huts in No 3 lines. The school had been established in March at Crowborough Camp. It ran four-week courses to train signalling instructors, the last of them at Seaford in November 1918, just as the war ended, and the school was disbanded the following month. The signalling school had been established because of heavy losses to line cables on the Front during 1916. This

All Saints Hospital, Eastbourne.

Sir Robert Borden addressing Canadian troops at Seaford.

was mainly due to shell damage and the signallers had to learn how to bury cables to avoid this.

On 11 August 1918, a church parade was held at the South Camp, Seaford. This was attended by the prime minister of Canada, Sir Robert Borden. Borden was a popular politician and a supporter of women's suffrage.

Early May 1919 saw one of the unhappiest incidents of the military occupation of Seaford in the Great War. On Saturday 3 May, Canadian soldiers at the South Camp, who were angry about restrictions being placed on them leaving the camp, disobeyed and assaulted their officers. They set about causing considerable damage to their recreation huts and canteens. The mutinous soldiers descended on Seaford next, indulging in what one resident described as 'general destruction and looting'. The East Sussex Police were unable to contain the men and called for assistance from London. The army established picquets both in Seaford and at the camps to deter or prevent disorder. A picquet is an advance line of sentries.

Details of the mutiny are scarce but it appears to have gone on for two days. The War Diary of the 3rd Canadian Engineers (Reserve Battalion) contain the following entries:

> *Saturday 3 May 1919*
> *Weather good. Picquet called out at night owing to a disturbance in town but not required.*

Sunday 4 May 1919
Weather wet. Disturbances in town and South Camp.
North Camp quiet.

Monday 5 May 1919
Weather good. Strong picquets in lines and in Seaford. No
disturbances.

Tuesday 6 May 1919
Weather good. Picquets in line and in town. No
disturbances.

Wednesday 7 May 1919
Weather good. Canadian Championship Sports at the
Oval (South Camp). Picquets in town and in lines at night.
No disturbances.

Saturday 10 May 1919
Weather good. Down town picquet. No disturbances

Sunday 11 May 1919
Weather good. Down town picquet. No disturbances

The riot is more vividly described in a history of St Wilfrid's School,
which was in Sutton Avenue:

One evening a howling mob smashes its way round the
town and is soon heard approaching the silent precincts
of St Wilfrid's. In the darkness, behind the front door,
stands Mr. Hall (one of the masters), a loaded 12 bore gun
in his hand, firmly resolved that if the place is to be
wrecked it shall not be without a struggle. Nearer and
nearer come the rioters, right to the corner of Sutton
Avenue, when, by the mercy of Providence, they turn off
in a different direction leaving St Wilfrid's intact.

Canadian memorial at St Leonard's Church, Seaford.

Americans

The training camps in Seaford were occupied by Empire troops, particularly the Irish, West Indians and Canadians. Many American troops went there to train as well. At least sixteen of the Commonwealth war graves in Seaford Cemetery belong to men who were born in the US or who were living there at the time of their enlistment. Britain declared war on Germany on 4 August 1914 but the US remained neutral despite enemy submarine attacks including the sinking of the *Lusitania* in 1915, when 120 Americans were drowned. The following year the cross-Channel ferry the *Sussex* was torpedoed en route from Folkestone to Dieppe and this turned many Americans against the Germans (see Chapter 3). It was very late in the day, on 6 April 1917, that the US declared war on Germany. America's neighbour had effectively entered the war with Britain in 1914. At the outbreak of war Canada only had just over 3,000 troops, but the Canadian Expeditionary Force was formed and thousands of men volunteered to join.

Many of these recruits were not Canadians but Americans – men like Walter Rauffenbart from Atlantic City, New Jersey. He was a plumber by trade but crossed the border and joined the Canadian Army on 21 February 1916, over a year before the US formally joined the fray. He had already seen service in the US Cavalry but died in Seaford, probably while undertaking training in April 1918. He is buried at Seaford cemetery near the grave of Sapper John Alexander, an auctioneer from Illinois who, like many of his fellow-soldiers, died when the influenza pandemic spread through the army camps.

Thirty-five-year-old Arthur Ardis was another influenza victim who is buried at Seaford cemetery. Although Arthur was born in Glasgow he had emigrated to the US and worked as a tram-driver in Massachusetts. Believing that his knowledge of the railway would be useful to the war effort, he travelled north of the border to enrol in the Canadian Railway Engineers in Montreal on 17 May 1918. He cannot have seen any action as within two weeks of enlisting he was sent to Seaford for training. He succumbed to influenza just a few weeks later on 27 July 1918.

Not all American fatalities at Seaford were from flu. Sapper Jack Berry of the Canadian Engineers was from Minnesota USA. He was a lumberman by trade and was probably an orphan as on his attestation papers he gave his next of kin as 'The Great War Veterans Association, Winnipeg, Manitoba'. He enlisted in 1918 but less than a year later, while based at the segregation camp in Seaford, he was struck by lightning and killed. New arrivals at a camp routinely spent twenty-eight days in quarantine to ensure that they did not spread disease or infection.

One American soldier buried at Seaford definitely saw action. That was 29-year-old Howard Jenkins from Iowa. He was a sapper in C Company of the Canadian Engineers and his death at Seaford in 1919 was attributed to 'pneumonia following gas wounds'. His grave at Seaford cemetery is inscribed, 'He played the part of a man in the Great War Drama.' Nearby is the grave of 20-year-old Jack Carr, a farmer from Washington.

Private Allan Thompson of the Princess Patricia's Canadian Light Infantry (one of the first regiments in the Canadian Army to see action in the Great War) was only 20 when he died of wounds at Seaford in 1918. He was from New Jersey but was born in Brooklyn. Other Americans buried at Seaford Cemetery are Private Samuel Burns, a rancher from Montana, 46-year-old Lance Corporal William Carrick of Houston Texas and 19-year-old Private Joseph George of Maine US.

CHAPTER 7

The War in the Air

Zeppelins

The military airship developed by Count von Zeppelin made its maiden flight in 1900. At the outset of the Great War the German armed forces had just seven airships, but the German Navy saw the potential and was keen to develop the use of airships. During 1914 they began reconnaissance patrols in the North Sea and early in the war, in January 1915, they were unexpectedly used to attack civilian targets on England's North Sea coast.

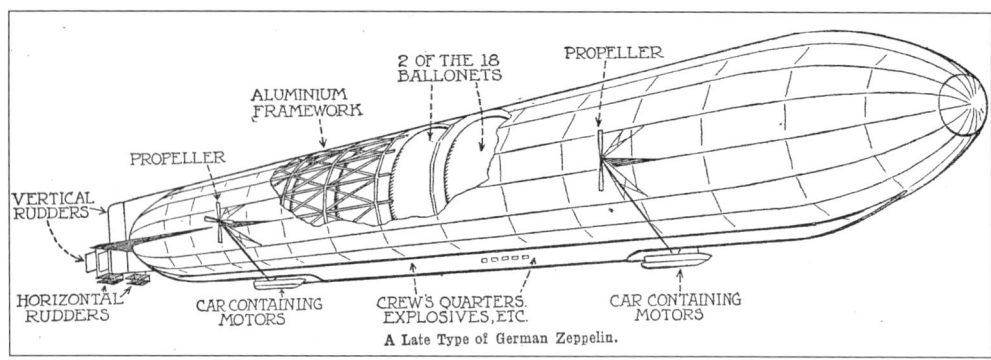

Zeppelin plan.

My great-grandparents, Ebenezer and Bessie Roberts, who lived in Eastbourme, were friends of the Beachey family who lived in Deptford. All but one member of the Beachey family were killed in one of the

Zeppelin bombing raids on south-east London on 8 September 1915. William and Elizabeth Beachey were poor and the whole family lived in an attic room. They were killed when a high-explosive bomb crashed through the roof. Only a 10-year-old girl, Lizzie, survived, waking up amongst the smoke and chaos, and running out into the street. My grandmother kept a scrapbook that contained a memento of this family tragedy, a silver and black-edged memorial card commemorating the Beacheys' death.

Across the south of England preparations were made for anticipated Zeppelin air-raids. On 4 March 1916 the chief constable of East Sussex, Major Hugh Lang, issued secret instructions to Seaford's new special constables. 'Should occasion arise, you will be at once called by the police, and I want you to proceed as quietly and as unostentatiously as possible to Seaford Police Station where you will be served with a warrant card, badge, etc, and remain there awaiting instructions.' Major Lang admits that 'the probability of a Zeppelin raid is remote. Owing to information received all necessary precautions must be taken ... Do not mention this to a soul, as I do not wish to cause unnecessary excitement among the inhabitants.'

Zeppelin postcard.

The airships were able to fly above the height that the early British air force could achieve. This great altitude also meant that bomb-aiming was highly inaccurate and this caused many civilian casualties. There was no predicting where the bombs might fall.

Because Seaford had two military camps these were later protected from air attack by large barrage balloons. Canadian Private Dobbs wrote home from Seaford in June 1917:

> *Our first night here was dark and rainy but the sky was pierced in all directions with searchlights looking for zeppelins. At noon today a heavy mist rolled up and the alarm was sounded upon which we all ran out and got away from the camp. We learned later that there had been a zep raid over the country but didn't learn of any damage done. There are lots of airships and dirigibles flying around here and we are getting quite used to them.*

Airship over Seaford.

Private John Cushnie wrote from Seaford in 1917:

> *We see a large number of aircraft around here –*
> *seaplanes, biplanes, observation balloons and what they*
> *call Fairy Queens, an airship which looks just like a long*
> *sausage up in the air. It is interesting to watch these*
> *aeroplanes manoeuvring about.*

The general fear of Zeppelin attack among the population as a whole was very understandable, especially after the horrors of the raid that killed the Beacheys in Deptford, but in the end there was no attack by airships on either Eastbourne or Seaford in the Great War. By late 1917 the attacks by airship ceased as the British military had developed better methods of identifying approaching airships and bringing them down. Then the attacks stopped, though only after 550 people had lost their lives.

Private Cushnie observed, 'During an air-raid there is just as much danger from shrapnel of our own guns as from the bombs of the enemy. You would think they would have a satisfactory method of dealing with the air-raids but these British people seem to be too slow to catch a cold.' If there were anti-aircraft guns, it is not clear where they were. Two batteries bearing sixteen guns in total existed just to the north-west of Exceat Bridge. They were aimed out to sea and were used for barrage practice, but they may have been used for training purposes only rather than intended for resisting a real air attack from the Channel.

Eastbourne Aerodrome

On Sunday 25 July 1909, Louis Blériot made his first flight across the Channel and just nine days later his fragile aircraft arrived in Eastbourne for a public display at the Devonshire Park. Eastbourne was determined to be a part of this exciting new phenomenon – aviation - and a few weeks later Eastbourne Council set up an Aviation Committee, which consisted of the mayor, councillors and local landowners. Within two years an aerodrome had been established by the Eastbourne Aviation Company between Eastbourne and Pevensey Bay (off Lottbridge Drove opposite where the Tesco superstore now stands). The enthusiasm of flying pioneer Frederick Fowler meant that

Eastbourne became a centre for aviation with both an airfield and an aircraft factory.

The *Manchester Guardian* reported on 14 August 1914 that flying from Eastbourne Aerodrome had been suspended as the entire facility had been commandeered for military purposes. Initially the site was used for re-fuelling and by the end of the year the aerodrome had been developed as an aircraft factory and flying school.

The factory used so much power that the Admiralty had to pay for a sub-station to be built nearby and for many aeroplanes for the Royal Naval Air Service and the Royal Flying Corps.

There was at least one wedding. Grace Simms of the Women's Auxiliary Air Force married Lieutenant Rundle-Woolcock at the Central Methodist Church in Pevensey Road on 25 October 1918. As the couple left the church, aircraft performed stunts overhead and dropped messages of goodwill.

The air-base was closed by June 1919.

Polegate

A Royal Naval Air Service was established in July 1915 near the Willingdon Triangle, a couple of miles south of Polegate. This was a base for non-rigid airships that were to patrol a vast area of the English Channel – particularly searching for enemy submarines. By 1918 the airships from the Polegate base were patrolling a very large area, 4,500 square miles, so sometimes the patrols were over twenty-four hours long. The Polegate base was the largest of all the airship bases, there being ten others scattered along the English coast. Most of the airships had the registration prefix SS, which stood for Submarine Scout.

On 20 January 1918, as they were returning to the safety of the Polegate base in a snowy gale, several airships collided near Jevington. As men rushed to the scene to assist, bombs exploded. But they continued their attempts to rescue crew members. In the end, there was only one fatality, Flight Sub-Lieutenant Swallow. He is buried at Ocklynge Cemetery. Three of the rescuers were awarded the Albert Medal for their bravery.

After the war the Polegate air-ship station was gradually run down. On 30 June 1919, there were five officers, thirty-nine other ranks, including fifteen WRAFs, but within four months this had been scaled down to two officers and twenty-two other ranks, though four men were kept on Beachy Head for providing weather reports. The Polegate airship station was finally closed on 6 February 1920.

Tide Mills

A Marconi Wireless Station was built on the beach between Seaford and Newhaven in 1906, close to the site of the former tidal mill. In May 1917 the Royal Naval Air Service established a seaplane base nearby on the beach at Tide Mills. The base was used to provide air cover between Dungeness and the Isle of Wight. With the formation of the Royal Air Force in April 1918 the seaplanes were designated as Flight 408 and Flight 409, and these in turn became part of 242 Squadron (along with a land plane unit at Telscombe Cliffs). The base consisted of two large hangars, workshops, stores, a pigeon loft and accommodation. There were also a few old railway carriages for use as offices.

When fully manned the squadron consisted of twenty-nine officers, twenty-three NCOs and 108 other ranks. There were also seventeen female military staff and seventeen female household staff: a total of 194 people. The assistant intelligence officer was Lieutenant Martin Press, whose job was to take charge of all the admiralty charts. He also had to keep up-to-date with the codes and submarine identification

Tide Mills sea-plane base.

signals and advise the pilots accordingly. Allied submarines had distinctive white markings on the top but also used coloured Very Lights, which were regularly changed.

Initially there were four Short 184 floatplanes and six Dover type 184 floatplanes, and these were later supplemented with Fairey Campania seaplanes. The wings of the aircraft folded back so that they took up less space when stored. The planes had two crew, a pilot and an observer who would have a Lewis gun and also be able to launch bombs. Typically the planes carried a 14-inch torpedo between floats or a 520lb bomb. They also carried two pigeons to communicate in case of trouble. The planes were equipped with radio, but it was primitive and only used for sending Morse code messages when in range of the base. By the end of 1917, six planes were flying from Tide Mills every day.

At the seaplane base there were also two tenders, a car and a motorcycle – used for the weekly run to the bank at Newhaven to fetch the wages for the base. In the summer the day started with the unpopular morning patrol, which left the base at 4.15am, after the pilot and observer had collected their sandwiches and a thermos of cocoa. The planes were armed and the safety pins of the bombs were removed. The planes were launched on an old railway buggy and pushed down to the water's edge, the pilot and observer jumping in at the last moment. The pilot used a system of compressed air to start the engine as the propellers were too big to start by hand. In order to launch it was useful to have a slightly choppy sea. If there was a mill-pond flat calm, the floats tended to stick to the water. Launches were not always successful and on more than one occasion planes hit the harbour arm at Newhaven. On 21 June 1918, Lieutenant John F. R. Kitchen and his observer George Cole were killed on their third attempt to launch in calm weather. They are both buried in Newhaven Cemetery.

Being made of wood and canvas the planes were prone to become un-airworthy if they got wet. Damage to the canvas was repaired by seamstresses, who were previously employed as sail-makers at Newhaven Harbour. At St Andrew's Church, Beddingham, is the solitary Commonwealth War Grave of Mrs Annie Piggott. It is unusual to see a Great War grave for a woman in England, let alone one from the RAF. Annie helped mend damaged aircraft – she was one of the first aircraft engineers.

A teenage Lieutenant Edward Ackery, who died as recently as 1990, later recalled his time on the Sussex coast. He regularly flew patrols from the Tide Mills base. The patrols were generally dull as they involved escorting merchant ships along the coast, to protect them from enemy submarines. This usually meant circling around the ships for hours at a time. On one occasion, as he was escorting a ship from Dungeness, Ackery's aircraft developed a fault. At Beachy Head he left the ship and flew on to Tide Mills but, as the ship rounded Seaford Head, it was struck by a German torpedo and sunk. Seaplanes scrambled to try to catch the enemy submarine, but it could not be found.

On 7 July 1918, Lieutenant Ackery was on patrol when he spotted a white torpedo track scudding across the water towards a convoy he was protecting. He was powerless to act but to his relief the torpedo missed the ships. Moments later the attacking submarines surfaced, oblivious to the air cover overhead. Ackery and his pilot attacked the subs. Aerial bombing was very primitive in those days. There were no bomb-sights and when bombs were dropped it was with heavy reliance on luck. Ackery felt a slight bump as his 112lb bomb was released and he peered over the side of the aircraft to see the bomb explode about 6 feet from the submarine. The crew were desperately trying to submerge. Oil was seen near the attack but in the excitement Ackery forgot to drop his second bomb, which might have secured a kill, which in turn would have meant a financial bonus for him.

The pilots were young and they were brave. They were feted as heroes and very popular with the girls. On one sunny day one of the Tide Mills pilots broke the monotony of his patrol by flying low over the beach at Brighton to exchange waves with girls on the prom. These antics were spotted by an officer. Later he was admonished by the area commanding officer who told him, 'There are no German submarines in Brighton Aquarium.'

Airborne heroes

It is difficult to single out individual men from the hundreds of brave local airmen who served in the Great War, but a handful of them should be mentioned.

Lionel Rees VC, MC, AFC, OBE, was a pupil at Eastbourne College. His exploits in the air over France and Flanders could fill a book. He was awarded the Victoria Cross following action on 1 July

1916, when he single-handedly engaged no less than ten German aircraft, despite being wounded in the thigh and running out of ammunition. He was reduced to throwing his empty gun at an enemy plane out of frustration.

Joel Hammond was born at Wanganui, New Zealand, and went to Wellington University. In 1906 at the age of 20 he decided to travel and make his fortune. First he went to Alaska to be a trapper, then he travelled to the Klondike Goldfields in Canada to be a prospector. He didn't strike gold. Then he was taken on by Buffalo Bill's Wild West Circus, where he worked as a cowboy – his horsemanship bringing him considerable fame. The circus travelled throughout Europe and it was probably when it came to England that Joel met his wife-to-be, 20-year-old Ethelwyn Wilkinson. She was born in Seaford in 1887, the daughter of William and Ada Wilkinson. Ethelwyn and Joel married at St Leonard's Church, Seaford in 1909.

While travelling in France, Joel saw Louis Blériot's new aeroplane and, being very much a man of action, he was soon flying. In October 1910, Hammond was granted an aviator's certificate by the Royal Aero Club, based in Piccadilly. He was only the thirty-second person to be issued with a pilot's licence in the country.

He took one of the planes, a Blériot monoplane called *Britannia,* back home to New Zealand and was the first person to fly in that country. He was employed by the government as their first pilot. He was also one of the first pilots in Australia and in 1911 flew from Perth to Sydney – a remarkable distance at that time. During this time Ethelwyn flew with him as a passenger and became the first woman in Australia to fly. In April 1911 she said, 'I always feel quite comfy when I am in the bi-plane with my husband. When we start it is only like being in an ordinary passenger lift, which has started a little bit quickly. It is a delightful experience.' When asked about her interests she said, 'I am especially fond of motoring, aviation and shark-catching.'

The following year Ethelwyn and Joel moved back to Sussex and Joel took a job with the Eastbourne Aviation Company. He was a flying instructor and flew exhibition flights from their airfield. He soon became very popular. In October 1912, *Flight Magazine* reported, 'Mr Hammond has taken a holiday and so has disappointed many people anxious to see his wonderful exhibition flights.' He kept his impish streak, buzzing golfers by flying low over Willingdon Golf Links, and racing trains.

At the outbreak of the Great War, Joel Hammond joined the Royal Flying Corps and took on dangerous missions over battlefields for reconnaissance work. He was such a talented pilot that when the US entered the war, he was asked to go to America to promote war bonds – as a sort of official stunt pilot. In September 1918 he attended the Fourth Liberty Loan War Bond Drive Air Display at Greenfield, but on his return his plane struck a tree and he was killed. It was rare for a flying ace to survive the war, but more surprising still that, having survived, he should die in a peacetime flying accident in America. Ethelwyn did not remarry. She died aged 64 in Hailsham in 1951.

Alexander Beck.

Alexander Beck was an Anglo-Argentine pupil at Eastbourne College, until he left in 1916 to become a vet. He joined the Royal Flying Corps aged 19. When his parents learned that he was in France they complained to the authorities that he was too young to be at the Front and he was recalled back to England. By this time – though still a teenager – he had flown thirteen patrols. He later returned to France where he was credited with bringing down eleven enemy aircraft. He was awarded the Distinguished Flying Cross and left the service in 1919.

Born in New South Wales, Andrew Cowper was another pupil at Eastbourne College. When war broke out he joined the Royal Sussex Regiment, transferring to the Royal Flying Corps in 1917. In just five months, between October 1917 and March 1918, he was credited with bringing down nineteen enemy planes. He was awarded the Military Cross with two bars. He died in Australia in 1980.

Andrew Cowper.

CHAPTER 8

They Did Not Fight

Conscientious objectors

Not everyone was in favour of the war. There were many who had political or religious reasons not to enlist. Some refused to take part in any kind of work that supported the war. These objectors became known as conscientious objectors.

In 1914 the Union of Democratic Control was founded, by the Liberal MP Charles Trevelyan and Ramsay MacDonald, who was to become the first Labour prime minister. A number of leading Liberal and Labour politicians and supporters joined the union, including George Cadbury, the Quaker owner of the chocolate manufacturing company, and Helena Swanwick, a Suffragette.

Charles Trevelyan travelled from his constituency in Yorkshire to address a meeting of the UDC in Eastbourne, but the Eastbourne police prevented the meeting from taking place after receiving a complaint from the local Conservative MP, Rupert Gwynne. Mr Gwynne certainly did not want such an anti-patriotic meeting to be held in his constituency, and he did not mince his words: 'I think it is most unfortunate that the government during the present national crisis should allow this gang of undesirables to preach their doctrine unfettered and undisturbed. I should like to see them all in gaol.'

There were about 16,000 conscientious objectors in Britain in the Great War. They fell into three categories. The absolutists, who were opposed to all forms of conscription and war work; the alternativists, who were opposed to military action but agreed to non-military work; and the non-combatants, who were willing to work for the military as long as they did not have to bear arms. 3,400 men took this third option, many of them working as stretcher-bearers for the Royal Army Medical Corps.

Quakers

A problem with objecting to fighting on moral grounds was that objectors had to demonstrate absolute consistency. In May 1916, the Eastbourne tribunal heard the case of Charles Seymour, an under-gardener who was a conscientious objector. He had previously attended the tribunal and had been granted a certificate of exemption. All was well until he assaulted a fellow worker, punching him in the face and knocking one of his teeth out. The military representative at the tribunal suggested that, despite his pacifist protestations, Seymour had proved himself naturally suited to the fighting line and was wasted in the Non-Combatant Corps. Seymour's certificate of exemption was withdrawn.

Other Quakers had a more prolonged experience. Fred Murfin came to Seaford as a prisoner and ended up being sentenced to death. Born in Lincolnshire in 1888, Fred later moved to North London, securing a job in the printing trade. He was a Quaker and was opposed to the Great War, or indeed any war. He knew his beliefs were unpopular and, following the passing of the Conscription Act in March 1916, he realized he could be arrested. He applied to a tribunal at Tottenham Town Hall for a non-combatant certificate, and was asked if he would kill a wild beast. He answered, 'Sir, the Germans are not wild beasts.' He was refused a certificate and, when a few weeks later he appealed at Westminster Guildhall, he was refused again.

On 21 May 1916, a policeman called to tell him he would be arrested in a few days' time. At Tottenham police station he was put into a cell with other conscientious objectors. They were evidently men of religious conviction, so the police did not bother to lock their cell door at night.

The following day they appeared at Tottenham Magistrates Court, where they were fined 40 shillings or sentenced to fourteen days' imprisonment. When they refused to pay the fines, they were marched to the nearest recruiting station, at Mill Hill, where they were handed over to the military. They were subjected to a medical. Fred refused to co-operate, so he was forcibly stripped and a khaki uniform put on him. The following day the COs were marched to Mill Hill railway station and sent to the south coast.

The authorities really did not know what to do with them, but their immediate destination was the North Camp at Seaford, to work alongside the 10th Border Regiment. An officer told them there would be no trouble for them if they assisted in running the camp. They would not be asked to fight but they would be expected to carry out tasks such as clearing paths, gardening and odd jobs. But Fred and his friends refused to obey any military orders. He later wrote, 'At Seaford we saw men having bayonet practice and throwing mock bombs. We saw one man who couldn't do bayonet practice and began to vomit badly – everyone could see that this practice was disgusting.'

On 28 May 1916, Fred found himself in front of a court martial for disobeying orders. The lieutenant dealing with his case had one arm and he told Fred that he had lost it while defending him. Fred indignantly replied that the officer had lost it while trying to kill another human being. This made the lieutenant very angry and Fred made the situation worse by telling him that he was not *Private* but *Prisoner* Murfin.

The next day Fred and seven other conscientious objectors were sent to France. Each was given a kit bag and a quantity of rations and equipment. When he was issued with a razor the quartermaster said he could use it to cut his own throat. They were forcibly put into puttees and handcuffed for their march to Seaford station. Another Tottenham Quaker, Stuart Beavis, refused to march and was roughly handled. His glasses were smashed and he was forced into a cart. At Seaford station they had a long wait for their train and the sergeant offered to take off their handcuffs, but the men refused. They wanted the people of Seaford to see that they were being punished for their religious beliefs.

Fred was taken via Southampton to Boulogne, where he endured appalling conditions and was subjected to another court martial. He was sentenced to death but this was commuted to ten years imprisonment.

The authorities' treatment of Fred Murfin, including his enforced expedition to France, today appears cruel and pointless. It was also inconsistent with government rulings of the day. Parliament had been told in May 1916 that, after court martial, conscientious objectors would be handed over to civilian courts. Yet, contrary to these assurances, the army had sent the men from Seaford, along with sixteen from Richmond and seventeen from Harwich, over to France.

The army continued to flout the wishes of Parliament and on 28 June 1916, Joseph King MP told Parliament that four more conscientious objectors, Privates Haywood, Bishop, Reccord and Fromow, had arrived at Seaford from Shoreham. All were members of the 4th Eastern Company (Non-Combatant Corps) of the 10th Border Regiment. They had not been court martialled and he feared they too would be sent to France. He said that the men were confined at Seaford in a room that was just 20 feet square and that they were released for only thirty minutes a day for exercise. Joseph King seems to have been a champion of conscientious objectors, asking repeated questions in the House of Commons concerning their welfare. He was a Liberal MP until 1918 when he defected to the Labour Party with his friend Arthur Ponsonby. Ponsonby lived in Sussex and established the pressure group War Resisters International in 1921.

Fred Murfin and the other men were later brought back to England. Murfin was taken to Winchester Prison where some of the Quakers agreed to serve with the civilian authorities. Fred again refused to co-operate and was taken to Maidstone Prison, where he was held until 1919.

Fred retired to Cornwall and in 1965 wrote a valuable account of his experiences as a conscientious objector for the Imperial War Museum. He died in 1972.

When Fred left for France he left behind many fellow COs who were alternativists. They agreed to work around the camp, keeping the place running. They probably had to endure constant verbal and physical abuse from the soldiers who were in the Seaford camps for training. In November 1916 the roof of a conscientious objectors' hut in the North Camp was tarred and set alight by Canadian troops. The ninety men inside the hut narrowly escaped being burnt alive in this attack.

The authorities tried to find work for them. In the latter part of 1916 they were loading transport ships at Newhaven. But in December 1916 the conscientious objectors realized that they were loading munitions. Over 100 of them refused to continue working. They were threatened with court martial, but it seems likely that they were found alternative work. In January 1917, 164 were employed mending the road between Seaford and Newhaven. Continually flooded, the road was certainly in need of repair. One flint wall built near the Buckle Inn had the letters CO picked out in flint work as a memorial to the conscientious objectors. Unfortunately it was demolished in the 1960s.

By October 1917, 1,037 conscientious objectors were deployed across the country on various construction works. They were paid 8d a day but of this 6d was deducted towards the army separation allowance, which was paid to their families. They were made to work eight and a half hours a day up to a maximum of forty-eight hours a week. In November 1916 there were allegations that the men were being given insufficient food for the hard manual work they were doing. The Secretary of State for War glossed over this. The mess unit of the camp hut had been inspected and found satisfactory, and no complaints had been made. It is doubtful whether the conscientious objectors were able to make representations to the inspection party.

The authorities often seemed to be confused about how to deal with conscientious objectors.

On 8 July 1916, Private H.W. Hampton of South London appeared before Dartford Magistrates and was handed over to the military, spending a night at Woolwich Barracks. He was then taken over to detention cells in Guildford, where he was forcibly stripped of his clothes and medically examined. Next he was taken to Newhaven, where he was handed over to the No 5 Eastern Company Non-Combatant Corps based at the Valley Camp. Two weeks later he was being guarded by members of the Royal Sussex Regiment awaiting a court martial.

Brothers John and Joseph Cornwell appealed to the Norwich Tribunal for dispensation as conscientious objectors, but before their case could get to court they were arrested and by 3 June 1916 were sent to a detention camp in Falmer near Brighton, where they were attached to the 9th Royal West Surrey Regiment. As they refused to work they were court martialled and sentenced to twelve months imprisonment with hard labour. Whilst at Lewes Prison their case was taken up in Parliament as it was discovered that their initial arrest had been illegal and their case was referred back to the tribunal.

Norman Thomas was a soldier based in Seaford. A letter to his wife dated 25 April 1917 gives a chilling insight into the relationship between the regular troops and the conscientious objectors.

There are a great number of "Conscientious Objectors" near Seaford; they have been employed for the past four months constructing one of the roads to Newhaven, the road is just the same as it was before the operations of the "COs". They were all allowed leave at Easter and Xmas and get real good food. Don't you think it is rather unfair to us fellows? We often pass them and pass a good deal of comments etc; sometimes there is a "rough-house" ending in a few COs being badly "mauled" and a few of us chaps escorted back to the Guard-room and then punished "C.B. etc." This is an everyday occurrence. I can see some fun here shortly if they continue to keep them here.

A CB punishment was being confined to barracks. It meant loss of recreation time and being ordered to carry out menial tasks such as scrubbing floors. The records do not show how long the Seaford camps hosted conscientious objectors, but they were clearly a source of irritation to the regular troops who were based there.

Today the wearing of white poppies to commemorate the suffering of the conscientious objectors still causes controversy. But it is clear from Fred Murfin's story that some of the men who, for ethical reasons, refused to fight were as brave as the next man. On 22 December 1916, it was reported to the House of Commons that 200 conscientious objectors of the Non-Combatant Corps had been working in no-man's-land between British and German lines, between Avencourt and Fricourt in France and that several of them had been killed.

In 2011 a peace garden was opened in Seaford, at the Crouch Gardens off East Street, by the actress Sheila Hancock. It was sponsored in part by local Quakers as a memorial to those men who courageously chose not to fight.

Peace garden statue.

Peace garden being opened by actress Sheila Hancock.

Seaford Peace Garden.

CHAPTER 9

Armistice and Remembrance

A school roll of honour

Ten days before the armistice, with the end of the war in sight, a service was held to commemorate the twenty-seven former pupils of the Seaford School (Infants Department) who had given their lives in the war. Hymns were sung and Lieutenant G. W. Downes gave an address. But the war was not yet over. A few weeks later the headmistress, Amy Chambers, was to write in the school journal that 'thirty-four laddies from this school have given up their lives for us'. Not twenty-seven but thirty-four. Another seven boys had died.

Armistice

On 11 November 1918, just before 11am, the soldier-author Arthur Baxter, then a member of the Canadian Military Engineers, was sitting in a hut at Seaford writing his novel when his thoughts were interrupted. He unexpectedly heard the sound of ships' sirens hooting across in Newhaven Harbour and out in Seaford Bay. He then heard a distant shouting and a cheer that rose to a crescendo and rolled across the town as thousands of people heard the news: THE GERMANS HAVE SIGNED!

News of the armistice spread quickly, people poured into the streets and lessons at schools were abandoned to let the children celebrate. The girls of Downs School sang *Land of Hope and Glory* 'with more fervour than it had ever been sang before', and one girl enthused that it was 'the most wonderful day the school and surely the world had ever known'. Most schools were given the day off and at Queenswood School in Eastbourne the girls gathered round the school flagpole and gave three cheers for the King, Marshal Foch and Earl Haig. One of the French teachers quietly invited other staff to visit her in the tiny telephone room with their toothbrush cups, which she filled to the brim with French wine that had been surreptitiously hidden away for the duration of the war.

The following day, 12 November, was given as a holiday at Downs School in Seaford and the girls spent the day making costumes for an armistice fancy dress dance that evening. The girls enjoyed a sumptuous supper followed by toasts to the King's health and the health of the army, navy and air service. A Belgian girl at the Downs School, Miss Bacon, wrote, 'Even the youngest of us felt that something oppressive had been removed from the air, for the first time the distant guns in Flanders were quiet at last, and for the first time in four-and-a-half years, peace had descended on the world again.'

On Armistice Day, flags were hoisted in the military camps, out in the town and all along the coast. Every shop, home and school displayed at least one Union Jack or some bunting. Very Lights were fired into the air. Regimental bands gathered to march through the street in impromptu parades and, as at churches all over England, the bells at St Leonard's Church rang out in celebration. Later the vicar of St Leonard's, the Reverend Frederic Cremer, held impromptu services of celebration, which were attended by several schools as well as local residents. It is possible that he also went up to the boxing arena at the North Camp as a big Thanksgiving Service was held there on Armistice Day. A postcard shows a vicar standing in the boxing ring, which had been bedecked with Union flags. This could be the North Camp armistice thanksgiving service.

Canadian soldiers gathered in the mess huts and one chap on the piano played the national anthems of all the nations involved in the fighting.

The following day Frank Cousins, a teacher in civilian life and now serving in the Canadian Cycle Corps, wrote to his mother with news of the armistice. He had seen action in northern France. 'The remarkable and long-looked-for day has at last arrived and the

Armistice Thanksgiving service, Seaford.

happenings of the past week are beyond my power of description. It is hard to realize that it is all over for me over here and the truth will not be fully appreciated until we reach home. But war is no more – in our time at least – and we can once more, in short, be human. Around me, many a tired soldier laddie, with a new look in his eye, says, "Thank God. No more damned soldiering for me".' He also mentioned that the Connies (conscientious objectors) too were in great glee at the news.

In the evening soldiers gathered in the pubs and streets of Seaford. Frank Clifford said that although Seaford was an 'eternally dead place', now there was a lot of excitement with 'much shouting, kids with tin bands, groups of wild soldiers'. That evening drunken soldiers could be heard shouting the toast, 'To the Allies and America.'

Official peace celebrations
On 1 January 1919, the mayor of Eastbourne, Alderman O'Brien Harding, held a public meeting at the Town Hall and called for

appropriate commemorations. The Mayor's idea was to found a club-house for ex-servicemen. It would be built 'on thoroughly modern lines' in the centre of town and provide various amenities including classrooms for the education of members. This scheme was rejected and instead it was decided that commemoration should include:

> a memorial (to cost no more than £1,000)
> a garden city to be built to accommodate war widows
>   and their families
> a fund to assist the widows and dependants of the fallen

The suggestions were formally adopted at a meeting of 21 March, and a seventy-strong committee was convened. The council appealed for funds, but by this time the town was war-weary and the anticipated donations were not forthcoming. Despite 9,000 appeal letters being sent to every household in the town, only £4,185 18s 6d was collected. The garden city scheme had to be abandoned, and in consequence some of the sponsors asked for their donations to be returned.

In Eastbourne the council officially celebrated the end of the war at the end of June 1919 and the Defence of the Realm Act had to be suspended in order to allow four days of 'full public lighting'.

Memorials

Almost every community in the country suffered loss. Out of more than 11,000 English civil parishes all but fifty-two lost men in the Great War.

Servicemen returning from abroad suffered withdrawal symptoms. Many found that they somehow missed the camaraderie and companionship of service. It was not long before old comrade social clubs were being established. In Eastbourne they also formed a football team – the Old Comrades FC – who are today known as Eastbourne United AFC.

These early associations were surprisingly left-wing and indeed at one stage it was mooted that ex-servicemen's associations should merge to become a political party. Lloyd George, the prime minister, had promised the troops 'homes fit for heroes' but after the war many of the men believed that the politicians had abandoned them. There were marches in London and the men found that they had an unexpected ally. General Sir Douglas Haig sided with his men and even refused an earldom until the plight of the men was addressed.

Peace postcard.

In June 1919, talks were opened in order to merge these groups and a few weeks later, on 19 July, along with the rest of the country, Seaford and Eastbourne celebrated Peace Day. There was a grand procession through Seaford. It was accompanied by the town band and virtually the whole population turned out – all in their Sunday best clothes.

In 1921 the British Legion was established. It was an amalgamation of four earlier societies, all of which had been set up to look after the welfare of servicemen injured during the Great War. These were the National Association of Discharged Sailors and Soldiers (formed as early as 1916), the National Federation of Discharged and Demobilised Sailors and Soldiers, the Comrades of the Great War (both formed in 1917) and the Officers Association formed in 1920. This last group was formed because officers were barred from joining the other organizations. Their membership was exclusively rank and file.

These organizations merged in May 1921 to become the British Legion. Haig was its first president and he devoted the rest of his life to the cause. He lobbied the government to provide funds and also ensured that injured men could gain employment, pressing for legislation to ensure that employers recruited at least 5 per cent of its workforce from the disabled community. Alexander Gordon benefited from this. As a Royal Marine he took part in the Zeebrugge Raid of 1916. He lost a leg but was sent to Eastbourne to recover and was given a job as a picture-framer at Stacey-Marks in Terminus Road.

1921 also saw the first-ever Poppy Day in Britain. It raised just over £100,000. The idea came from an American nurse called Moina Michael, who established a Flanders Field Poppy Day in 1918.

Seaford was one of the very first British Legion Branches having been established on 2 August 1921. A photograph shows the remembrance day parade possibly in 1922 arriving at the Alfriston Road Cemetery. The parade is headed by a number of sailors who, despite their youth, are wearing medals. Behind them are men carrying a banner: Seaford Branch of the British Legion.

Within months of the armistice steps were taken to remember the fallen by erecting memorials. The British Legion was central to the campaign to remember the fallen.

Memorials took a variety of forms from the grand memorial at Eastbourne to small plaques on the walls of churches and schools. Some memorials took a more practical form, like the Memorial Hall at Alfriston. At St Mary's Church, Eastbourne, the memorial takes the form of a covered walkway connecting the church with the parsonage. At St Peter's, East Blatchington, the war memorial was a new organ.

Memorials were erected in offices, police stations, fire stations, post offices, clubs and factories. In Eastbourne a wooden war memorial was erected in the entrance of the police station in Grove Road. It remembers the five officers of the Eastbourne Borough Force who never returned to their beat at Eastbourne. A similar memorial was also erected at the main Eastbourne Post Office but has since been moved to the depot in Southfields Road.

Eastbourne police memorial.

Seaford War Memorial (in its original position in Dane Road).

On 3 May 1921, many Seafordians gathered in Dane Road for the unveiling of the Seaford war memorial, a Celtic cross in Cornish granite. The site was close to the former fire station in Green Lane and is now occupied by the loading bay for Morrison's. The memorial lists the names of 104 local men who lost their lives.

Following the Second World War the memorial had to be brought up to date with the addition of more names. The new masonry was cut in 'imperishable letters' by Bridgman Ltd and the monument was put in place by Stevens Ltd, both local Seaford firms. Most of the funds to move the memorial were raised by the British Legion. With this renewal it was decided to move it to a more visible location at a place known to Seafordians as the cats' cemetery, at the junction of Sutton Park Road and Avondale Road. This spot is still the focus of the Remembrance Sunday parade every year and the town flagpole stands nearby. A rededication ceremony took place on Sunday 2 November 1952.

A further war memorial was erected in Seaford in 1922 at St Leonard's Church. It is made of Sicilian marble with a gilded cross and a palm leaf with the dates 1914 – 1918. It has no inscription beyond the ninety-three names of the fallen. Seaford Museum is now the home to several displaced war memorials, including that of the Seaford branch of the Ancient Order of Foresters. Sixteen of their 'brothers' were killed in the Great War.

In all more than 100 Seaford men lost their lives in the Great War – and this from a population of only 3,800. This equates to 2.5 per cent of the population of the town.

The first Seaford casualty of the war was Lieutenant Commander Clement Head, the son of John and Charlotte of 'Highlands', Seaford. Clement Head initially trained as a pilot and received an Aviator Certificate (Number 191) flying a Bristol bi-plane at Salisbury in March 1912. During the Great War he joined the submarine service. He died in December 1914, while in charge of Submarine D2, which was lost in the North Sea with a loss of all twenty-six of its crew. The submarine was rammed by a German patrol boat near the island of Borkum off the German coast.

In Eastbourne 1,065 men lost their lives through war service, the equivalent of 2 per cent of the town's population. The Reverend Henry Plume MA carefully gathered their names, which were then carved on sixteen oak panels. The long row of panels recording the names can still be seen in Eastbourne Town Hall. The memorial panels were unveiled on 1 November 1920 by General Lord Horne GCB, KCMG. General Horne was the only Artillery Officer to lead an army during the war and is known as the architect of the creeping barrage. After

Eastbourne war memorial is unveiled.

visiting the town hall ceremony he walked to the end of South Street for the unveiling of the main war memorial. This was a bronze figure representing the Angel of Victory mounted on a stone pedestal. It was designed by Henry Charles Fehr, a distinguished architect who was responsible for memorials in Hull and Leeds as well as the figures that decorate the Supreme Court in Parliament Square.

All of Eastbourne's ex-servicemen were invited to attend the unveiling of the memorial, as well as the Blue Boys from the Summerdown Camp, nurses and ambulancemen, army cadets from five local schools and girl guides and boy scouts. Invitation cards decorated with Union Jacks were delivered to all the families of the men who had died. Two hundred and ninety children orphaned by the war marched from their schools to the site, where a crowd of over 4,000 gathered. Windows overlooking the scene were occupied by injured ex-servicemen to give them a view of what was believed to be the largest gathering of people the town had ever seen.

A service and speeches were followed by Last Post played by buglers from Eastbourne College. After a march-past it was the turn of the public. One-by-one, widows and others who had lost friends and relatives left wreaths so that at the end of the day the whole area was a field of flowers.

School memorials

Seaford and Eastbourne were renowned for their schools and dozens of schools in the towns lost old boys to the war. Seaford College was evacuated to Petworth in 1940, but the school chapel there still has a smart brass war memorial listing the twenty-four boys who were killed in the war.

Eastbourne College lost over 160 former pupils to the war and headmaster Edward Carleton Arnold raised a massive £48,000 for a huge memorial building designed by former pupil Geoffrey Cecil Wilson. The building dominates the college site. A few steps lead to an undercroft, which contains a memorial listing the names of the fallen old Eastbournians.

The preparatory school for Eastbourne College was called Ascham St Vincents and after the war a memorial arch was erected at the front of the school in Carlisle Road recording the names of the fifty-one former pupils who died in the war. The school closed in 1977. The memorial arch survives, though the names on the memorial have suffered weathering.

Some of the school memorials have been lost. The brass memorial for St Wilfrid's School was unveiled in 1921, commemorating two old boys, Donald Pearson, who was drowned when his ship HMS *Marmion* sank off the Shetland Islands in 1917, and Neil Robertson, who received the Military Cross and bar and was killed in action in northern France in 1918. The school was demolished in 1981 and the present site of the memorial has not so far been traced.

Some school memorials were lost but later recovered. An example is the heavy brass war memorial at Bowden House School in Seaford. A few years ago it was found propping up a bath. It was carefully cleaned and restored and has now been placed on the wall of the reception area of the *new* Bowden House School.

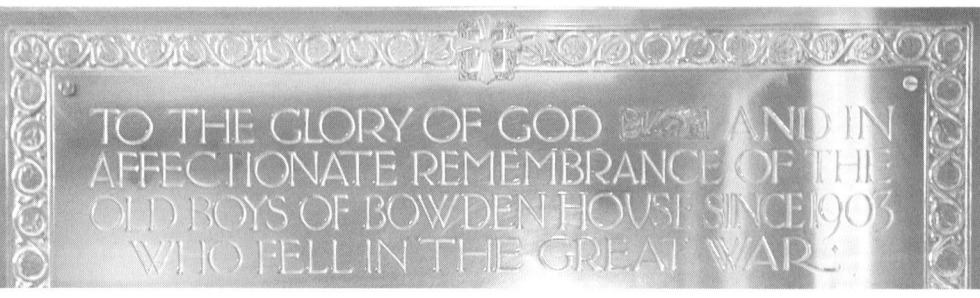

Bowden House school memorial.

The Treaty of Versailles

Although the armistice was signed on 11 November 1918, the war was not formally concluded until the Treaty of Versailles on 28 June 1919, exactly five years after the first fateful shot of the war in Sarajevo.

Gradually the servicemen were discharged and allowed to return home, some more quickly than others. Mr Gwynne, the Eastbourne MP, lobbied Winston Churchill for the release of two local men in May 1919. He said that Corporal 21225 Tappenden of the 306th Road Construction Company, Royal Engineers, and Lance-Corporal R. V. Herriot of the 309th Road Construction Company, Royal Engineers, were urgently required back in their former jobs by Mr Thomas Gurr, a brick maker at Polegate. Churchill said he would enquire into the case.

Medals

Unfortunately, it would not be possible within the pages of this book to list all the casualties and the names of all the recipients of medals awarded during the Great War.

Not everyone was awarded a medal. Arthur Baxter who had listened to the sounds of the armistice while stationed at Seaford later commented that he had not been decorated for his war service because he was 'neither sufficiently forward – nor far enough back'.

My grandfather Alex Gordon's name was put into a ballot to receive a Victoria Cross. This may sound improbable, but following the action at Zeebrugge in April 1915 the men taking part were deemed to have been so brave that Admiral Sir Roger Keyes invoked Rule 13 of the Victoria Cross regulations. This allowed a ballot to be held and, from Alex Gordon's ship, Lieutenant Commander George Bradford was selected. My grandfather received the three standard medals, the 1914/15 Star, the War Medal and the Victory Medal, but my grandmother was always proud that he came so close to receiving the Victoria Cross.

The exceptional bravery of Major Cuthbert Bromley and Sergeant Major Nelson Carter resulted with Victoria Crosses. Bromley was from Seaford, the son of Sir John Bromley of Sutton Corner. In 1915 Bromley led an attack of a heavily defended beach at Gallipoli. A naval bombardment had failed to clear the enemy but Bromley's men managed to take the beach under withering gunfire. He died later in the war whilst at sea and has no known grave. A road in Seaford is named after him and there is a brass memorial to commemorate him at St Leonard's Church.

Nelson Carter died on 30 June 1916, when he led an assault on enemy lines at Richebourg l'Avoue in France. He took an enemy machine-gun position but was killed whilst he was assisting a wounded man to safety. He was buried nearby. Before the war Carter was a commissionaire at the nearby Old Town Cinema, and after his death the cinemas in Eastbourne gave benefit performances that raised funds for his family. In 2007 a blue plaque was placed on his home in Greys Road.

Cuthbert Bromley VC.

The next-of-kin for personnel who had died on war service were sent bronze memorial plaques. Although much larger that a coin, each plaque became known as the dead man's penny.

Nelson Carter blue plaque, Eastbourne.

The design shows Britannia and a lion. Also included in the design are two dolphins, to remember the maritime services, and at the base a lion eating a German eagle. In all, over 1,355,000 of these were issued along with a printed scroll with a facsimile signature of King George V.

A special service
Two days after Remembrance Sunday another service is held at Seaford, not to commemorate local deaths but to commemorate the soldiers of the Commonwealth who died in the Seaford training camps.

Commonwealth ceremony, Seaford.

A memorial listing the men resting at Seaford Cemetery lies many miles away in South London. On Remembrance Sunday 2006, St Peter's Church just off Clapham High Street was packed to commemorate the West Indian soldiers who died on the south coast. A host of dignitaries was present, including His Excellency Emmanuel Cotter, the High Commissioner of St Lucia, the Canadian Military Attaché and Rear-Admiral Peter Wilkinson of the Ministry of Defence. After a brief service the congregation moved to the nearby headquarters of the British West Indian Ex-Serviceman's Association (WIESA) where a striking slate memorial listing the names of the soldiers at Seaford Cemetery was unveiled. The Fevrier family from the West Indies, traced by WIESA, attended the service, and two days later they were able to see the graves of their ancestors, buried at Seaford Cemetery: Nelson and Dennis Fevrier, who died in January 1916. The Fevrier family were touched to get such a warm welcome from the people of Seaford.

The last survivors
The last surviving British soldiers of the Great War. 111-year-old Harry Patch and 113-year-old Henry Allingham, died within a few days of each other in 2009.

In 1991, Mrs Winifred Mandeville of Mercread Road, Seaford, died aged 94. In 1917 she had joined the Women's Army Auxiliary Corps and was soon sent to Pont De L'Arche near Rouen in France. Winifred was there for two years and got used to the hard life amongst wounded soldiers and German prisoners-of-war. Interviewed in 1988 she recalled a big push in 1918 when bread was scarce and she had to live on huge solid maggot-ridden biscuits that were so hard they had to be broken with a hammer. She remembered that on Armistice Day both she and the German prisoners-of-war stood to attention and wept.

William Gregor was one of the oldest members of the Seaford Royal British Legion. He had been a sapper and later a corporal in the Royal Engineers before being captured by the Germans in 1918. He suffered appalling conditions but managed to escape by jumping out of a cattle truck whist being transported towards Germany by train. After many adventures he eventually managed to cross back into allied trenches – but only after being fired upon by both sides. William died in 1990 aged 94.

Over the last few decades, the surviving participants of the Great War have dwindled, slipping away, one-by-one. Even the longest-lived survivors have gone now. The stories of Seaford and Eastbourne in the Great War have slipped from the realm of memory into the realm of history.

Wreaths at Seaford Cemetery.

Bibliography

Periodicals

Contemporary newspapers accessed from the British Newspaper
   Archive

The Eastbourne Herald, The Eastbourne Chronicle and *The*
   Eastbourne Gazette

Hansard

Municipal Eastbourne 1883 to 1933

Illustrated London News

Sussex County Magazines

Summerdown Camp journals

Daily Mail Year Book

Books

Arthur M., *Symbol of Courage*. (Sidgwick & Jackson 2004)

Carew D., *Many Years, Many Girls*. (Browne & Nolan 1967)

Cundell F., *Jamaica's Part in the Great War*. (The West India
   Committee 1925)

Elliston R. A., *Eastbourne's Great War*. (SB Publications 1999)

Fellows P., *Newhaven Seaplane Station 1917-1920. (unpublished)*

Grieves K., *Sussex in the First World War*. (Sussex Record Society
   2000)

Hide T., *The Pleasure Boatmen of Eastbourne*. (SB Publications
   2007)

Hide T., *The Fishermen of Eastbourne*. (SB Publications 2009)

Hymans M., *A History of Eastbourne Buses*.

Larn R. and Larn B., *Shipwreck Index of the British Isles*. (Lloyds
   Register 1995)

Longstaff-Tyrell P., *A Picture of Polegate*. (Gote House 2004)

Lowerson J., *A Short History of Sussex*. (Dawson 1980)

McMahon L. and Partridge M., (*Eastbourne Aviation Company 1911-1924*. Eastbourne Local History Society 2000)

Pugh P., *The Grand Hotel*. (Grand Hotel 1987)

Smith R., *Jamaican Volunteers in the First World War*. (Manchester University Press 2004)

Spillane P., *St Andrew's School 1877-1977*. (St Andrews 1977)

Surtees J., *Barracks, Workhouse and Hospital* (Eastbourne Local History Society 1992)

Walsh J., *Seaford Golf Club – A Short History*. (Lindel Promotions 1986)

Index